What can I say

to a friend with cancer?

What can I say

to a friend with cancer?

Randy Becton

Christian Communications
P.O. Box 150
Nashville, TN 37202

Published by Christian Communications
A division of the Gospel Advocate Co.
P.O. Box 150, Nashville, TN 37202

ISBN 0-89225-320-7

ACKNOWLEDGEMENTS

I want to express my gratitude to two groups: the Primetimers (formerly 39'ers) and the Hiway 36 church for their belief in the work of the Caring Ministry. J. B. Phillips describes the compassion of these Christians when he translates Hebrews 13:3—"Think, too, of all who suffer as if you shared their pain." Through gifts, prayers and volunteer hours, both groups "share their pain." I affectionately dedicate this work to my father, H. E. Becton, Sr., from whom I have learned much.

PREFACE

I marvel at the way God uses people. The mysterious way in which God moves redemptively is more clearly seen in the life of Randy Becton than in any other person I know. His sensitivity and compassion and empathy are refined by the fires of his own personal suffering. He is a man who is well aware of the fear and loneliness that comes in the dark night of the soul.

And yet Randy is a man who inspires faith and hope and love—God's eternal verities. I have seen him reach out to hurting people when others wanted to do so but for some reason hesitated. I have seen him minister to people who are suffering physically and who are suffering spiritually. The two are not readily separated into neat, nice categories when we're fighting for our very survival.

Randy is a dear friend. He is the kind of man with whom I would risk anything. God has made him that way. There are many people who feel the same about him, even those who scarcely know him. However, Randy cannot possibly be in all the places he is needed and wanted. God has also blessed Randy with the gift of writing as a means of multiplying his ministry of caring.

What follows is one way of sharing his healing words of comfort and affirmation. These letters are from ordinary people—like you and me. People who are hurting and lonely and frustrated and sometimes full of despair. They are wondering where God is in all of their troubles, much as any one of us would. In Randy's responses, we have in a concrete way a sense of his presence, his caring, and his insightful words of advice. In so doing, people are helped and God is glorified. My prayer is that God will continue to use Randy Becton to touch the lives of countless thousands who are wondering where God is in all their troubles and whether anyone cares.

Royce Money

CONTENTS

INTRODUCTION:

Brother of All Who Suffer

For 13 years it's been my privilege to try to comfort cancer patients and their families. My own battle with cancer, and my mother's battle before me, made me sensitive to the unique loneliness and struggles which patients face. I recall a quote:

> "Whoever among us has, through personal experience, learned what pain and suffering really are belongs no more to himself alone. He's the brother of all who suffer."

I really feel that if I have a gift, it may be the gift of sensitivity, of caring about hurting people. Human suffering always strikes me as individual, unique, and important. My heart, really since childhood, has hurt when a person experiences real pain in his life, whether that pain is caused by a fractured relationship, a blocked dream, feeling like a "nobody," or the experience of serious life-threatening illness. In this book I am writing about those who suffer from cancer.

I've learned that being sensitive is not enough. To care means more than to feel. Caring involves entry—entering into another's pain. Helping to bear the load and ease the pain is a vital part of caring. At the heart, caring means presence, assuring a hurting human that he is not totally alone.

Entry into others' pain requires more than desire. To truly be helpfully present, I must become an equipped person; I must learn something about helping others through their sorrow or pain. Centuries of books have addressed suffering. My anguish centers in my own inadequacy. Simply put, I don't know how to care for a suffering person in ways most conducive to healing. To be a brother to one who suffers, I must desire to understand exactly what the cry of his heart means and meet him in ways that open possibilities for service to his soul. How can I share confidence and faith with one who needs the very touch of God himself. It's not easy.

When I became sick, I learned how quickly a person's emotional and spiritual strength ebbs under the assault of poor health. I met face-to-face the horrible loneliness. Fear became more than a concept; it was a teeth-rattling reality in the long, dark hours of the night. The only real surprise, I suppose, was the sheer power of fear and loneliness to drown hope and the confidence that one is loved and cared for. My confession here doesn't suggest that faith and hope have no chance in tragic circumstances, for they do. But in addition to one's own faith, it is important for someone to be there with us in these moments. Without someone to touch you when you feel abandoned, you may sink beneath the dark waters of fear never to emerge again. You can hold your breath under water only so long!

Someone may suggest, "You're being too dramatic, Randy." Or, "Well, that's ideal but it's not always possible to be there for another." Let me tell you, I hope when your crisis occurs someone will be there for you. You had better pray for one person who seeks to be present, seeks to understand, seeks to comfort—yes, even seeks to be a visible reminder of God's love for you.

Without that person, your chances of survival aren't as good as you may think.

Now, I hope I have your attention. In the following pages I have sought to tell you what cancer patients and their loved ones have told me. Because we want to help them, we must first understand the dimensions and seriousness of their problems.

Through this book I try to share with you the hearts of some sufferers. As you read their emotions and feelings, you will be moved, just as I was. My goal involves more than being moved. I believe you really care and sincerely want to be effective in meeting the needs of those who suffer. So we will enter their hearts in an attempt to understand better—to gain equipment to be more effective brothers and sisters to them. In truth, everyone wants Jesus at his side when he hurts. The one called Christian is asked by his Lord to be "Jesus at his side" to a suffering person. This is our Lord's eager expectation. We, his followers, don't go alone. He goes to the side of the sufferer through us. Suffering persons in your future will say to you—"I understood more of God's love for me when she served me" or "I felt God's care when he was there."

For us to make progress in faith, we must go deeper. First, we must go deeper into the life and ministry of Jesus to understand more fully our Great Physician. Secondly, we will want to go deeper into the lives of the suffering to see the style of ministry, the ways of helping, that are needed and available. These letters and my responses are intended to help us go deeper, to learn more, to become more skilled in giving care. Remember, we are Jesus at the side of the sufferer.

As you read these letters, listen with all your heart to what they are saying. Those who wrote them deserve to be heard. They see what suffering *actually is*. These are not words which they mouth about suffering as an idea or concept. Sufferers would give all they own if you and I, their brothers and sisters, would try to understand what they are experiencing. Very few who suffer think they do it well. Almost no one would say, "Here is how I am suffering, and I am doing well at it."

Perhaps I am speaking here on behalf of those who have written me as well as myself. Most of us know how others would have us suffer. We also know how we would prefer to handle our own suffering. But what matters is the truth—what is *our* suffering experience. The letters which I share in this book are characterized by a total vulnerability—an openness—which tells the good as well as the not so good. The candor that the sufferers show came from their feeling that I could understand. Something that I had written or said made them think that I might understand what they were going through if they put it into words.

My editing of these letters has taken hours because of my commitment to preserve the writers' privacy. I hope we can listen with the heart and learn to equip ourselves to be Christ's servants among people who suffer. I invite you to listen.

Listening is both a gift and an acquired skill. It grows out of a sincere desire to know and understand. Real listening hears both the feelings and, deeper than the feelings, the reality of the situation. The listening heart of the Christian hears compassionately, hopefully, redemptively. I listen to you as a precious person. You are unique; what happens that hurts you is also unique. Your perspective on your suffering is important. More important, though, is the bearing of Christ on your suffering. We must remember that because of Christ, suffering has taken on a new meaning. Also, because of him, I listen to you differently than I might have. I really care about you, for you belong to him. Jesus teaches me how to listen to you by letting me observe his life.

That's why I study carefully how he dealt with people, especially hurting people.

Jesus was especially good at allowing people to describe their own situation in their own way. He listened for the cry of the heart which went deeper than the words. He gave people a new vision of what to do with their fears, anxieties, guilts, anger, insecurities. That's how we know he understands everything we experience. Duncan Buchanan in *The Counseling of Jesus* shows how Jesus dealt with people.[1]

The good news is that Jesus' life, death, and resurrection forever change the nature and meaning of human suffering. It is also true that those whose lives are changed by Jesus comfort their fellow sufferers in a new way: they serve in the spirit of Christ. My comments after these letters seeks to give concrete glimpses of what the spirit of Christ involves.

SUFFERING AS TEACHER 2

At the very beginning, let me caution you against thinking that God allows suffering simply for the "lessons" we can learn from it. Sometimes that can be true, but there are other important reasons why suffering is a reality in our world. (I discuss these fully in the book *Does God Care When We Suffer.*

Suffering can have positive values in our lives, but that is not the same thing as making a blanket statement that suffering is good. Please, let's be more sensitive to the horrible, difficult, undeserved, and unexplainable suffering that affects so many lives. God is not happy about human suffering. Let's not be glib about other people's suffering. At the same time I believe that suffering people must place their own meaning (if there is to be *any* meaning) on their individual experience of suffering. Any benefits or uses of suffering must be arrived at by the sufferer himself who reflects on his life and his faith, especially his faith.

Now to some of the lessons that sufferers have learned from their experience:

Suffering as character builder. Runners use sprints and long-distance runs to make various muscles strong for their particular races. In a similar way the effective handling of trials makes a stronger person, a more disciplined person—one with a strengthened spiritual fabric. Earlier non-biblical Christian writers referred to this as "soul making." The "refiner's fire" images of suffering in Scripture carry this idea. Suffering believers whom I have known have used their experiences to draw closer to God, to refocus their lives spiritually, or to learn a level of surrender to God's will which they had not known previously.

I must emphasize this is a choice because for one person suffering may result in a stronger faith while another may allow suffering to embitter him against God. To be clay in the hand of the potter, someone said, you must climb up onto the wheel. Paul said in Romans 5:3-5 that "we also rejoice in our sufferings, because we know that suffering produces perseverance; perseverance character; and character, hope."

Believers who profit from their suffering accept it with a willingness to grow. They don't deny what's happening to them or run away from it. They examine suffering and seek to see how God can work through it. In Romans 5:4 the word "character" describes gold tested in fire and soldiers who prove themselves in battle. Believers have confidence that God is working in their lives, making of them the children of God in whom He is pleased to dwell. Paul declared that God desires "to conform us into the image of His Son" (Romans 8:29).

Suffering as correction and education. According to the scriptures, God allows suffering as punishment. Certainly this is not always true, but it is mentioned occasionally. Sometimes the guilty are punished; sometimes not. But sometimes the innocent suffer also. A person can examine his life for a "chastening" effect and perhaps profit from it. Suffering can be the occasion for self-evaluation. There's no question that this is often helpful.

Suffering as a gift to others. Suffering can be used for the good of others. I've always thought of 2 Corinthians 1:3-4 as a suggestion that we who receive God's comfort in our affliction are then equipped, to some degree, to comfort others in their afflictions. Suffering can be the occasion for a ministry to sufferers. We can turn some of our interests to others who hurt, learning in that action something of Christ's self-giving love.

This is a brief look at ways suffering can "teach" us. Again, however, these uses of suffering must be conscious choices for they are not, in any sense, the natural fruits of suffering.

NADINE: *That Troublesome Anxiousness*

Dear Randy,

I'm crying out again this morning while the whole world sleeps and I'm here alone. Dr. W. called me Thursday and is putting off my trip for the bone marrow transplant. He's putting me back in the hospital Monday for six more days for another bone marrow biopsy and another round of chemotherapy so I won't go out of remission before the transplant. I don't know the reason for the delay unless they are afraid because of my age. I've been so upset and confused, crying and wondering, "Why?"

I wanted to go on and get this over with and get back home. Maybe this delay is God's will to help me as much as He can with this dreaded disease. I am not usually a crying or complaining person, because I know God will not put more on me than I can bear. But just the thought of being back in the hospital on Monday and more pain and chemotherapy was more than I could handle tonight. You know how it is when you've been through so much, and sometimes it seems the drugs and transfusions and platelets and doctors are all in vain. But I know through God's hands Dr. W. is fighting for my life.

I know the best remedy for discontent is to count our blessings from our Lord. He knows and understands all things. I appreciate somebody understanding the loneliness of this struggle I'm going through. I try not to let my true feelings show to my dear husband and the girls. They have held up so good under all this and I know the pressure on my husband is really great. Pray for him to bear this with me. He is a Christian and believes in our Lord so truly and faithfully. We have been married 32 years and he just won't even think of being without me. This is the strength he needs now. I pray for God to stay with him.

Here is a little prayer I'm learning to say over and over: "Teach me, Father, when I pray not to ask for more; But rather let me give my thanks for what is at my door. For food and drink and gentle rain, for sunny skies above, for home and friends and peace and joy. But most of all for love. In Jesus' holy name I pray, amen."

I feel much better now. The dawn is breaking through—another sunrise, another gift from God. I am so blessed. God has led me to have so many new Christian friends whose love and concern for me is so great even though we've never met. I feel almost as if I've been talking with you. It helps. Our dear Lord is so great and we aren't alone. He will never leave us or forsake us.

Sincerely,

Nadine
Mississippi

Maybe it is true that the difference between fear and anxiety is that fear has a focus while anxiety is a state of worry in which a whole series of "maybes" or "perhaps" pervades our attitudes, frightening us. Many sufferers find themselves unable to sleep because they have specific worries and a general uneasiness about their situation. It's easy to be anxious when everything that is precious to you is threatened because of one reality: a life-threatening illness. Our personal future has a dark cloud over it and everything is on hold. In some sense we have lost the ability to control anything, and there's no wisdom in making plans that we fear we won't be here to fulfill.

Perhaps those people who advise us not to worry forget that in similar situations they would also be burdened with worry. To know that you can't change the outcome by worrying doesn't automatically stop the worrying. Aren't we being truthful if we admit that underlying our worries is the fact of death? If it's true that the reality of death is always just beneath the surface, coloring all our attitudes and activities in life, then how much more so when you have the occasion to face it up close—with time to mull it over. The fact is death, but the real question is faith.

God asked us to be His children—a relationship in which fear is ruled out and love is the new reality. Fear, therefore, must be put to death again and again in the person of faith. I believe human fear is understandable and not surprising at all in life-threatening illness. Its presence is a last vestige of the natural man—the unredeemed sinner—before we accepted God's grace. Remember, Scripture says we were "in lifelong bondage to the *fear* of death" (Heb. 3:15).

As Christians, I believe, we are given new realities to defeat death and the fear of death. These are: (1) a relationship—that of God's child, (2) a power—that of

His Spirit living within, and (3) a hope—that of resurrection. These realities, brought to memory and allowed to control our thoughts, beat down the fear again and again. I believe the Spirit of God helps us beat down fear by testifying to our spirit that we are in fact God's children. In other words, God helps us tell ourselves the truth about ourselves (because of what Christ has done). This word from God defeats fear. That's why I encourage Christians to discipline their hearts to dwell on *who their God is* and *who they are because of Christ*. Remember, Jesus reinforces his concerned disciples, "Fear not, little flock: for it is your Father's good pleasure to give you the Kingdom" (Luke 12:32). He's saying, *Trust God. He is trustworthy!*

There's no point in saying "don't worry" to suffering people because it doesn't work. Remind your friend who God is—that He is in control and He loves and cares for us uniquely. Then stay near this person so that by your care he is reminded of God's care. Read with him God's promises and urge him to be sure to pour out all his feelings to God in prayer. He can tell God exactly how he feels and be assured that God under and understands. If he is angry with God, that doesn't offend Him—He knows the reasons the sufferer is so frustrated and feels so helpless. Encourage him to list all his reasons for wanting God to "see it his way." The Father wants to hear. Of course, sufferers will feel better about themselves if they pray with a worshipful heart, in gratitude for His goodness, and if they ask for a heart willing for "thy will to be done, not mine." Jesus cried "unto Him who was able to save him, and was heard for his godly reverence" (Hebrews).

Nadine reminds us that the struggle is lonely but that in all the matters we wrestle through, we can be sure that we are not alone. The God whom we serve doesn't forsake His own.

I like what Phillip Yancey observes about Jesus when he says, "Even God in the flesh, Jesus, reacted to pain much the same as we do. He recoiled from it, thought it horrible, did his best to alleviate it, and finally cried out to God in despair because of it." If sufferers can remind themselves of this truth, they will not feel so totally alone and will know that God understands, cares, and is there. Since Jesus "put a face on God"—or showed us exactly what God is like—we can know His closeness in our dark hour.

KAY: *Four Stressors*

Dear Randy,

I have Hodgkin's Disease. As you know, this is cancer in the lymph node glands. I was diagnosed in March of this year. On Monday, March 4, I was sitting at my desk when I found a lump in the left side of my throat. On Monday of the next week I was scheduled for a biopsy. Then the following week I went back into the hospital for all the tests. I also had surgery where they did various biopsies and removed my spleen.

I went back in August for a check-up after my radiation treatments. At that time we found another node under my arm. I had it removed August 19. I am presently going through radiation.

My biggest battle is keeping my feelings in—for you see, my mom and dad are both sick and I try not to let them know how I feel. Mom has back problems and is easily depressed and Dad had Lupus (which is a disease of the blood).

My husband is very supportive and is so good to

help. I have an 8-year-old daughter. I try to talk with her as much as she can understand. But her main concern is, "Mama, are you gonna be alright?" I know you know what I mean. It's hard to talk about it—and it's hard when people don't really know what you are going through.

My strength is the Lord—I pray each day He will give me strength to take another treatment and to keep going—you know. I know now what "living one day at a time" means and how important it is to trust in the Lord. We just have to continue to trust that He will heal us and that we will be stronger as a result of what we are going through.

I think the scariest part is not knowing what is ahead and how it all affects us and our loved ones. You know I have to wonder, "Why?" when everything is great, seems as if we are happier than we've ever been—then the next thing we know I have cancer and our whole life is different. I think my first thought was, "Why me?" Then, "What have I done to deserve such a rock in the road?" Then I turn and think, "How does the Lord plan to use me through all of this?"

Sometimes I get so tired—I just want to go to sleep and pray it will be gone when I wake up; but I know that's not possible so I just try to continue to be strong and fight.

Love in Christ,

Kay
Mississippi

Having cancer is only part of the problem. When we must deal with the "realities" that surround the cancer experience, we encounter such pressures that the stress can become heavier than a 50-pound sack of coal on our back. We deal with possible treatments, what the likelihood of a cure will be, the real possibility that it has spread too far—that nasty word *metastasis*—and that's just the beginning. Sociologists who study cancer patients tell us there are four psychosocial stressors found among cancer patients. Patients must deal with:

(1) *Reconstructing reality.* Each patient must deal with the "new reality" and find ways to cope with the imagery surrounding cancer. The new realities can include pain, disfigurement, hospitalization, doubts, job loss, disability, and death. How a patient responds to his or her diagnosis determines the content of this new reality of being a cancer patient.

(2) A *new understanding of the preciousness of time.* We can have "unfinished business" that we feel an urgency about. Our interest can turn to living a fuller life "one day at a time." This lady is in her early thirties and, with an eight-year-old daughter, wonders about the length of her life. She still wants to talk of her "future"—her next wedding anniversary, her child's graduation from high school. Primarily she is interested in being a *survivor.* Her life must now include computed to-mographic scans (CT), hematology visits, treatments, and blood work.

(3) A new need to *manage uncertainty.* There are problems associated with the cancer experience that demand solutions. Some of these include: (a) maintaining a normalcy in lifestyle in the midst of a medical crisis, (b) controlling symptoms, (c) adjustments in relationships because of being a "cancer patient," (d) adapting to the ups and downs of the course of the illness, and (e) finding money to finance the treatments and sustain a household.

There are unique unknowns and uncertainties to which doctors, family, and friends must respond.

Sometimes, too, cancer patients can't tell if they are making progress toward remission or cure, or if they are going downhill in the battle. Patients, like everyone else, desire to remain autonomous and productive in life. The greatest stress comes in the area of beliefs, attitudes, and values. A lot of sorting out of priorities takes place. Cancer seriously challenges long-held beliefs; and emotionally-charged feelings are difficult to cope with successfully.

Patients usually ask one of these questions regarding time: Am I going to recover from this? What can we do to get me well? If I don't get well, how long do I have? These questions concern time. Our goals and hopes for life make these questions crucial to us. If we are not going to live, there is a move to "settle our affairs" or "finish unfinished business." It's very important to realize that if a person gets a negative answer to the question "Will I get better," his interest in self-treatment or some alternative to conventional medicine will grow. Patients seek to regain control. They want to do something other than surrender or resign themselves to death.

(4) *Coping with pain.* Some researchers say that one-half of all cancer patients cope with moderate to severe pain. Some deal with chronic pain which can assault the human spirit. Feelings of meaninglessness, helplessness, and hopelessness are associated with this problem. In short, pain assaults a patient's self-image because it eliminates feelings of assurance and well-being. Uncertainties increase because of pain.

These four stressors are formidable, but what's important is that we recognize them and their effect on the morale of the patient. I believe that better understanding of these stressors can help sufferers apply their faith to their experience. Also, those who seek to encourage patients must know the realities they cope

with in order to move alongside them as encouragers.
To encourage Kay, a person should:

(1) Believe with her that her treatments are going to arrest her disease.

(2) Pray to that end.

(3) Encourage her to be open with her feelings, especially to God in prayer.

(4) Remain silent to anyone else about any of her feelings of doubt or despair.

(5) Reserve until later the temptation to dwell on consolation about heaven and our final victory over death through Christ.

JOY: *No Substitute for Presence*

Dear Randy,

I'm writing concerning my 74-year-old father. He is a faithful Christian and was diagnosed as having metastatic adenocarcinoma. It began apparently in the pancreas and has spread to the liver and intestines. We believe his lungs may also be involved.

The doctors (who have been terrific) believe his time is only a matter of months. His pain seems pretty well in control at this time, but he is so weak he sleeps a lot of the time. He is at home and plans to stay there as long as possible. There are no plans for chemotherapy or radiation.

My major concern is my mother. She seems to be doing real well under the circumstances. It is hard for me not to be there with them. The church is being very supportive and a day never goes by without visitors.

Dad has never found it easy to express his feelings. He has been able in this to discuss financial matters and take care of needed business, but it has been real difficult for both of them to open up their real inner feelings. Any help that you can give would mean so much.

Love in Christ,

Joy
Arkansas

Sufferers who write me almost always mention the *power of loving presence* as a great help to them in their suffering. In difficult illness the natural inclination is to shrink back from physical presence with the sufferer. Maybe it's because we don't have good answers to the "why" questions. Perhaps it's because of the unpleasantness of being around sick or dying people. For some the sights, sounds, and smells of hospitals bring back painful memories of earlier sad experiences in their lives. Whatever it is, it is not unusual for people to shrink back from personal involvement with those who suffer. We want to *care*; we just don't want to *go*.

I'll admit there are bad times to visit. But that's not the point. The point is that sufferers need to see the *visual* expression of God's love in a caring person who makes himself or herself *available* to them. There is no substitute for this. Sufferers testify that those who help them most are those who come when needed, listen more than they talk, touch and hug them, and even laugh and cry with them. When we serve in this way, sufferers can actually see and experience how much God loves them. They can know God will not forsake them by watching you and me accept and love them. We send a message consistent with the nature of our

God: we're going to go through this suffering *with you*. This presence speaks powerfully; it has great therapeutic value, often bringing peace and calm to a troubled heart.

Sufferers aren't looking ultimately for good answers for their head. They are looking for someone who will be a true friend to their hearts.

You may know that some Jewish people practice a custom called *shiva* after a death in the family. For eight days friends and neighbors join the mourning family in their home, providing meals and conversation. Most of all, they are present, participating in the loss, "grieving alongside" the family. The wisdom of the custom is that it reverses the natural tendency to avoid another's pain. Rather, it declares that we will make your pain our pain. This truth is central to the Christian who would minister in Jesus' name. That's precisely what He did.

Sufferers don't always require our presence, but they do appreciate our finding ways to tell them that we care and are with them. A covenant of prayer for the sufferer is one important way. Regular notes or other expressions of concern help. Notice I said *regular*. I encourage you to find your way to be there. Work extra hard not to abandon sufferers whose illness takes a downhill course. You don't have to know what to say. When you go, they are keyed in on your heart—not your words. It's emotionally difficult for anyone to be there, but this only underscores that there is no substitute for presence.

C. S. Lewis, in *A Grief Observed* (a beautiful journal he kept after his wife's death), says that sufferers are tempted to think that God has abandoned them. He can seem distant, even absent and unconcerned.[2] Sufferers can see Him, in this dark hour, perhaps best through a member of the body of Christ who is physically present.

This is sometimes hard to understand, but grateful sufferers assure me it is true.

MRS. ROBERT A.: *God Helps Rebuild*

Dear Mr. Becton,

It is very difficult to adjust when a part of my body was cut off. My husband and I were well-tuned and we functioned well together. We were one. Now I don't have him. I am missing him a lot and I must rebuild to fill that gap. I am here because God put me here for His purpose, so I trust in Him and follow His direction.

For the last five months God filled all my needs with countless miracles. People might say that it just so happened that way. But I believe that they are all God's miracles. Every little thing fit together like a puzzle board. It is just a beginning, and I am sure it takes many years to see the complete picture. As a matter of fact, it takes my lifetime. But I can see a glimpse of a little part of the picture here and there now.

God is good and I believe in Him. He is my total source and strength. God sent many angels to help me through this difficult time. I don't have any blood relatives in this country, but God provided me with many wonderful friends who genuinely are concerned for my welfare and helped me. Every sweet and comforting word is like medicine to my heart.

Sincerely yours,

Mrs. Robert A.
California

No one does a more graphic job of describing the pain of losing a loved one than Mrs. R. A., when she declares that "a part of my body was cut off." She still treasures being Mrs. R. A., for she and he were one with each other.

She is grieving in a healthy way. She knows that an important part of her task in grieving is to turn from the fact of the loss to forge a meaningful new life. This is not a time for despair but for new life. She knows God has purpose for her and she is grateful that He has surrounded her with loving friends. They are a reminder to her of His care. She reaffirms her faith in God, although she's still aching, and she sets off for the future with her hand in His.

I have an idea that Mrs. R. A. will be an effective comforter to others who mourn the loss of their mate. She meets her pain honestly, grieves genuinely, then turns toward a new day wherein God will supply meaning.

DOROTHY: *A Living Faith*

Dear Randy,

Praise God, we are not alone. Last year on this date I entered the hospital and was operated on for a knot under my arm. It was cancer, lymphoma. It took a lot of praying before I could completely turn it over to God. When I did, I was a new person, because I don't think about this enemy—for God can control or remove it.

My love for God grows every day more and more. There's no life without God. The word "cancer" alone can destroy you, if you let it. We have a thorn in the flesh.

I go once a month for check-ups. I have swollen glands, but so far I need no medicine or chemotherapy—but I may have to one day. I pray for strength *daily* because I need it. We have a *time to go; our* worry is to *be ready*. If we turn ourselves completely over to God, He will remove our worries.

I don't think about cancer because I'm in God's hands. I pray to stay in God's care. Praise His name!

In Christ,

Dorothy
Tennessee

After the shock and horror of the initial diagnosis, Dorothy thinks through her circumstances carefully. Cancer is her enemy but she re-evaluates her faith and decides she will not allow it to destroy her. She determines that the best thing to call her illness is a "thorn in the flesh." Like the apostle Paul, she prays for its removal but will not let its continuing presence dominate her. She reaffirms God's sovereign control over the universe (and disease) and is content to pray for strength on a daily basis. She believes God's will is going to be done in her life. Her attitude reminds me of Paul's statement, "whether we live or die, we are the Lord's."

Dorothy was ready when her time to go arrived. Like other sufferers with a living faith in a living God, she now loves Him in His presence. That which was faith and hope for her is now sight and reality. Her faith in the midst of suffering teaches us that those who ultimately win are those whose confidence rests in God.

MAROLYN: *Who Can I Tell How I Really Feel?*

Dear Randy,

I am a 33-year-old mother of two small children, ages 5 and 9. I have a wonderfully happy life and still consider myself basically a happy person even though I lost a breast to cancer two years ago.

I have always considered myself basically a strong Christian; however, lately I feel myself grow weak. I feel that upsets my close friends whom I confide in. They feel I am about to lose my faith. I don't plan to do that even if I live to 100. I'm too close to home. But I do feel it's my privilege to feel weak sometimes if I want. I was so encouraged to read in one of your books that I am normal and it's okay sometimes to be weak.

You see, two years ago when I had surgery the surgeon told me I had only one positive lymph node. I was sick to know it had gone that far, but oh so encouraged. I *knew* I would beat it with God's help. I prayed that I could still lead a normal life while on chemotherapy and still take care of my family. I *was determined*. I would work a few minutes, lie down and rest for 5-10 minutes, get up and go again. I did almost everything I had done before. I went on family outings when my head ached and probably missed no more than four or five church services while on the drugs for a year and a half. My blood counts have always been low with elevated billi rubin, so the methetrexate was in small amounts.

I have been very tired so I went back to the surgeon and asked him to go over the pathology report with

me (as no one ever got around to it). How stunned
I was to learn the lymph nodes affected were four
and not one. In breast cancer this is a terrible
difference— the difference between recovery and
death.

Then came the setback. Not only the setback, but the
symptoms. (I had some before, but was so optimistic
as to dismiss them as something else.) I'm disturbed
with myself, because it seems I trusted the Lord to
be bigger than the cancer and one lymph node, but
He can't handle four. My prayer life hasn't been
what it should be lately, either. It seems like I'm
always fussing at Him. I am dizzy for days at a time,
hurt in the center of my stomach, and have back
aches. Also, I have an enlarged liver and spleen,
with constant infection in my tonsils.

There have been no lumps to come up yet, but I
know it is a matter of time. The doctor (oncologist)
is non-commital, trying to be encouraging. But
eventually—after being lied to once—I know he's
trying to give me hope because he doesn't realize
I've done my homework (I read a lot).

I feel like everyone is trying to keep me in the dark.
Why should everyone else know more about your
physical health than you do yourself? That's mighty
personal. I asked if he recommended I go to M. D.
Anderson and he feels it's not called for. So I sit and
wait, keeping my condition mostly to myself and
one or two very close friends. Maybe that's not wise,
but I choose it that way. I don't want to be treated as
"sick."

You have to admit that others treat "sick" people
differently. Can you imagine how they would treat a

terminal person? I had one girl who always patted my arm with this sympathetic look of doom in her eyes. Even though I love her and appreciate her Christian concern, it drove me up the wall. I wanted to be treated as normally as possible for as long as possible. Maybe by then I will be better able to cope and much more adjusted. So, of course, *this letter is confidential.*

You know, Randy, I don't fear what comes after death even though I am in awe to think I will stand before the Lord. I know I am a Christian and I was never so sure of my salvation as I was those early days in the hospital. So why do I dread death? I *grieve* over my 5-year-old son who most probably will not even remember his mother. I ache for my 8-year-old girl who will not have the chance to be a little girl before she is thrown into the real world of housework and responsibilities. I grieve for the husband I leave behind. I grieve because my life is a vapor. It appeared for awhile and leaves only smoky memories and a faded photograph. I'm even kind of jealous to think of the possibility of my husband giving his love to another woman, even though I know it would be the right thing to do and I certainly don't want him to live a lonely and miserable life. Isn't that silly? But it's real.

It all boils down to the fact that I'm trying to walk by sight. Where, oh where is my faith? (I'm even considered a very strong Christian by my friends.) This is the biggest mountain I've ever climbed and right now I'm not doing so hot.

Thanks! I guess I just needed to talk with someone I knew would understand. I know my life will serve some purpose and it has already, but I know I'd rather glorify the Lord in life than in death. I know that's selfish, but that's how I feel.

Sincerely,

Marolyn
Mississippi

You can easily see from Marolyn's letter that patients fear what others will think of them as they battle serious illness. Many have told me they were afraid their family or friends would be shocked or disappointed in them if they should express their *real feelings*. This feeling, whether valid or not, contributes to a sense of isolation and loneliness. "Who can I be myself with?" Marietta doesn't want to be treated as a sick person, with people making special concessions for her or condescending to her. She especially feels that she can sense if someone responds to her as a dying woman. This fear probably matches her own inner apprehension about that possibility.

In our rugged individualistic society we are taught to endure our fears silently and to keep our hopes and aspirations to ourselves. Many do this to save embarrassment. Others don't want to burden people with their problems. Still others want to protect their family and friends from being upset. Maybe we're afraid people will decide we're not very good Christians. Some psychologists have observed that holding in our feelings can be detrimental to our body. They also suggest that we fail to develop the tools to deal positively with the emotional aspects of illness. In short, we cheat ourselves and live in a "pretend" state. In several situations I have known, the critical need was for honest, open communication of real feelings.

Perhaps we have felt we were in pretty good control of our emotions most of our lives. Suddenly there is serious sickness which threatens our self-image and even the quality of our relationships. A patient thinks, "I'm no longer a healthy, active, in-control person; now I'm a cancer patient." Patients respond healthily when we encourage them to say, "This is how I feel; this is what I'm thinking." I've wondered why so many cancer patients write articles or books or later speak about their experience. In part the answer could be their quest to understand what has happened to them and to express how they really feel about it. They seek to have this horrible experience make sense. Further, these people may be seeking to find ways to make their suffering experience useful to others. Many use group therapy for these reasons. I've heard patients say the following:

1. "My having cancer has alienated me from my husband. I really resent him for treating me this way, even though he must be going through a lot, too."
2. "I'm so mad at God. I don't know why I ever believed in Him. He's so cruel to us. He just plays with our lives."
3. "Why does everybody pretend with me. I see the look of death in their eyes when they look at me."
4. "I'm scared silly. I guess I've never really been a Christian. Every time I think about what's happening to me, I get so frightened that I think I'll go out of my mind. I'm so ashamed."

What's sad about these expressions is not that people verbalized how they felt. The sad reality is that they felt there was no one who would really understand. We all like to think that we are compassionate, non-judgmental people. But are we? Perhaps we want to say something like this to a sufferer:

I really want you to feel free to talk to me. I'd like that very much. When you're ready, I'm available to listen. If you want to cry, that's fine, too. I may cry, too. If I were in your place I'd want to have someone to share my thoughts and feelings with. We've had good times—we can share this, too. Maybe through sharing God will help us get through.

Perhaps a note communicating this message will be effective. Whatever the method, sufferers wait for signs that someone will care in this way.

Dr. Neil Fiore suggests three skills necessary to deal with complex emotions: (1) the skill of *framing* difficult feelings, (2) the skill of listening to understand, and (3) the skill of speaking about how we really feel in a positive, helpful way.[3]

We can frame difficult feelings gently by saying things like, "This is really hard for me to say because I'm afraid you'll misunderstand and be hurt, but I feel . . ." This helps a person prepare for your feeling. Another way: "I have this feeling that I'm not comfortable with. Maybe you can help me. I feel . . ."

We can develop listening skills by holding back quick answers, being slow to give advice, avoiding pointing out flaws in the other person's thinking, or trying to convince another to change what they are feeling. Our goal is understanding, not winning. Sufferers often describe how they feel about their problem, but they don't do it so we can solve it for them quickly. Truthfully, they're talking to be *heard as persons.* We really can't remove their dilemma. We can enter into their pain. If we offer understanding rather than advice, they will sense our spiritual support and gain courage to cope with their suffering. So many times the problem won't go away. Sensitive listening can help them gain renewed strength to confront the problem. Sensitive listeners are made, not born. We can learn to do it better. We can learn to "paraphrase back" what we hear rather than "interpreting" or "correcting."

We will want to speak about how we feel in a positive manner. We can learn to be assertive in a "you win, I win" manner that lets no one lose dignity or self-worth. Many good books on active listening are available. One I recommend is *The Ministry of Listening* by Donald Peale.[4]

Notice, especially, Marolyn's fear of losing relationships. With her death her children might not remember her. She thinks these fears are abnormal, but they regularly flood her mind. Her faith struggle is real. She really wants to trust God with what might happen, but she is afraid because she is not in control of her own future. She trusts her thoughts to someone whom she thinks understands these longings. That's why a non-critical listener, who will share his own vulnerability about mortality and expose his own "weak" faith, is the person who can best encourage her. John Drakeford's book *The Awesome Power of the Listening Ear* describes the kind of listener she needs.[5]

PEG: *What A Difference Jesus Makes!*

Dear Randy,

I truly do feel as if I'm writing to an understanding friend! In November of 1970 I gave birth to my third precious son. Our home was a small, idyllic community in the Southern California mountains, where my husband was captain of the fire department. There was much love in our family. I built my life upon and around my roles of wife, mother, and homemaker.

Four months later my world crashed in around me with the words, "You have cancer." My diagnosis was lymphoma, in advanced stages. Every circumstance and condition that I had depended upon in my life for security, identity, purpose, and fulfillment simply crumbled to dust.

My nursing child was (almost literally) snatched from my arms; my other children were cared for in the homes of friends (thank God for them, though). My husband grew strained and burdened meeting everyone's needs and struggling with his own fear, grief, financial stress, and exhaustion from frequent trips up and down the mountain (the distance was two hours from our home to the nearest radiology facilities).

My new role became "cancer patient." I was terrified, bitter, confused, depressed, angry, (you know, the usual). I had always believed in God, but I was alienated from Him now by the thought that He must be *real* mad at me. Oh, the unspeakable pain of what seemed like total aloneness! Doctors too busy to talk, nurses too uncomfortable with the subject of cancer (death, of course, their *true* fear), family and friends forcing cheerfulness and talking all around the "big issues," me pretending to be "strong" so as not to upset them more, and on and on. . . . Ugh!

During the next three years I had radiation therapy nearly everywhere in my body, and then a few months into remission I broke out with the shingles on my face and they spread into my right eye, causing blindness in that eye and severe scarring on my forehead. I can't describe the pain of that— physical pain that overshadowed the next two years.

Several months later, my husband left us. I began

taking more pills to relieve the pain of heartbreak, too. I got staph and strep several times and spent several months in the hospital. I consented to having my boys go live with their dad and his new wife. With the last shred of my reason for living gone, I had a complete emotional breakdown and ended up back in the hospital. Well, that was the beginning of the beginning. . . .

Somehow Jesus touched me there and began to draw me up out of the miry pit. It was a long, slow climb (five years) and I kicked and screamed and struggled all the way. But in January '78 I accepted His glorious gift of grace and yielded my life to Him completely. Now, here's where I run out of words. The peace that passes understanding also defies description—but, you already know. Praise His name!

I've had chemotherapy in some form for more than five of the past seven years (in fact, I'll be mailing this en route to the doctor's office today). The new life that Jesus has given me (and all three of my sons—alleluia!) is full and fragrant and sweet. My security, identity, purpose, and fulfillment all rest on the solid rock now. I am growing in the grace and knowledge of our Lord Jesus Christ and looking for His soon return.

This letter has been uncomfortable to write because I don't often dredge up these hurtful memories any more, but I realize with renewed impact what a drastic turn-around the Lord has brought to my life, and the stark contrast of black despair with the light of His blessed hope. Thank you, Jesus!

In the love of Jesus,

Peg
California

The power of words to express what is in our hearts is evident in Peg's letter. Her diagnosis caused her world to crash in, and she sought to sort out the differences between security "because life goes well" and security "in spite of it all."

In the face of unbearable pain, she found a new power to cope through Jesus Christ. I'm reminded of Corrie ten Boom, who spent years in Nazi prison camps and in her later years wrote of the power of faith to overcome suffering. She tells of visiting a patient suffering unbearable pain. She told him of being humiliated in the concentration camps by having her clothing stripped and being forced to stand naked. She found comfort in remembering the amazing love of Jesus who willingly suffered for us on the cross. Suffering patients often look forward to the day when they will be free of their suffering. Passages such as Romans 8:18 and Revelation 21:4 bring comfort to those in great pain.

Often the faith of the sufferer provides a blessing to the person seeking to give comfort. Peg's faith blesses me. She is so thankful to be in Jesus that his light gives her peace, even though she suffers. Peg discovered the key to making sense out of suffering. She came to know the Lord over suffering—Jesus Christ. He was known as the Man of Sorrows, and he understands how sorrow and suffering threaten us. Human history makes sense when it is seen as His story—He came to us, as God-with-us, beginning in a stable. He went all the way to the cross—experiencing suffering for each of us—and He left an empty tomb to prepare a place for us. That's what suffering believers depend on. They also believe that one day he will dry every tear and empty every tomb because his love is stronger than death.

"He will wipe every tear from their eyes, and death shall be no more, neither shall there be mourning nor crying nor pain any more, for the former things have passed away . . . I will make all things new . . . these words are trustworthy and true." (Revelation 21:1-5).

Peg believed the One who made these and other wonderful promises and committed her life to Him. In Christ, she has overcome. All of God's promises are summed up in Jesus Christ.

STANLEY: *The Weight of a Broken Heart*

Dear Randy,

Since I lost my daughter in 1984, my heart is as close to being broken and still alive as possible. We had gone through 13 years of chemotherapy for leukemia, had two remissions and finally lost Becky to pneumonia. Becky was 17 when she died, a junior in high school and a member of the honor society. She was our only child and we couldn't have had a happier and fuller relationship.

Since her death I have not been able to make any sense out of all of this and I'm surprised at how weak my faith is. I've seen so much suffering of innocent children for so many years that the image of a loving God is too much for me to accept any longer. Becky suffered for so long that I can't comprehend anything that could justify this kind of existence. It's not enough to be told only, "You have to have faith." I think I deserve more.

I miss my Becky so much sometimes I don't know which way is up. I know my wife feels the same. We keep very busy and that allows us to go on day after day. But I keep expecting something to change—so far happiness is still gone and we only become harder instead of more accepting.

My attendance at a support group for bereaved parents helps, but I'm still looking for some strong understanding to allow me to accept this lousy situation. I know I sound like some spoiled cry baby and I really don't care because I have to have a better way of living with this than I have right now. I would really like to be able to lean on my faith so much more than I can right now—but I really don't expect anything now after how abandoned I feel by my God. I have prayed so much so many times for mercy for Becky. I looked hard and saw so little. How I wish I would have seen more. I am hurt real bad and don't expect to understand soon. But I still seem to want to keep trying.

A Broken-hearted Father

My life and work gives me the opportunity to see into the hearts of others. Often I feel inadequate to meet their needs, but always I am confident that God has no inadequacies and that if I can point these hurting hearts to Him they will find the way to healing.

But Becky's father is different!

Becky's father wrote me, searching for lost hope. His letter touched my heart deeply. Because of his letter I appreciate my beautiful, healthy 18-year-old daughter more intensely. I want to help him. I want to share God's love. But I can't. Let me explain.

People often write to me when they are in confusion or pain. But sometimes they forget to include the address where I can reach them. On occasion amateur detective work reveals a way to get in touch with them. But often writers of such letters remain mystery persons who will never know that I got their letters and I cared. In these cases I rely on prayer and a caring God to meet their needs without my help. However, Becky's father haunts me. I want to take a further step toward him and others who hurt like he does. Maybe Becky's father will see in this printed page a glimpse of the answer he seeks.

The letter reminds me of Francis Thompson's poem, "The Hound of Heaven." It's about God's pursuit of a reluctant soul. This father sounds as though he is considering abandoning faith; but I don't believe God will let him go. He talks about feeling "abandoned . . . by my God" and how he keeps trying to understand. It may help him to understand that his preoccupation with trying to understand may be an indication that God has not abandoned him. God is trying to draw him near.

I think God cries, too, over letters like this. After all, God made Becky. He knows her better than her father does, and He loves her more, so it must have been anguish for Him to watch Satan attack her. Artists love what they create. If somebody comes along and ruins the creation, they grieve. God must be even more attached to His living works of art.

God is crying with this father. But God has demonstrated His care by doing more than shedding tears. He gave a Son to die willingly to defeat the power of sin and death. The final word is not death but, because of God, the final word is LIFE.

I think, too, that this father is grieving over his lost faith that had all the answers, his lost world-view where the good guys always win. That's in addition to his grief over his daughter.

Let me share with you a letter I wrote to Becky's father. I was seeking to respond to one whose heart is broken.

I read your letter when it first came, and I have reread it several times in the days since them. It is powerful and has powerfully moved my life as it opens a window onto your world and the heaviness of your heart.

I have wept and given thanks all at the same time. I am thankful that you are a skillful communicator and a genuine human being with great capacity for joy as well as sorrow. I rejoice in the life which Becky lived. She was the center of your joy, for sure.

I know a little about grief, but no one really understands another person's grief. And I don't understand yours but perhaps a flicker. My heart goes out to you in gratitude that you are honest with your feelings. God understands and respects that. Your letter didn't disturb me, but rather it tells me some matters go deeper, to matters of the soul.

You are in touch with your feelings and with the harshness of suffering in the world. Beyond that, you have the capability and willingness to be in touch with a God whose nature is loving.

There are really two choices for you as you respond to Becky's death. The first is bitterness and despair, taking that hollow place in the marrow of your bones and looking at it only as darkness, with no meaning and no possibility of providing light or hope to any other human being.

Another choice is available. You can press toward life with the decision to love and to serve others as a "wounded healer"—someone who has been significantly hurt and who uses that understanding to move close to other people in their own pain so that they do not feel alone. You can serve those who hurt because you understand their pain.

I know a little about this second choice because I was diagnosed with a life-threatening illness at the age of 29, having three children under four years of age. I've seen some of the darker side of life and I would be among the first to say that it's not easy. In fact, I would quickly say that it hurts badly.

But I would add that life is a gift from God. He's the only one I've found who has shoulders big enough on which the losses, brokenness, and shattered dreams of life may rest. I've looked for permanent promises in broken people, but the promise of meaning for my life I have found from God, my Father.

When I ask "Where is God when it hurts?" I find the best answer is His own suffering, the giving of His own Son. (I'm speaking here of Jesus' death on the cross.) His death speaks to all human suffering. It is a raw decision of faith to select Him. But it is a life-giving choice rather than a death-dealing choice. I believe that love is stronger than death. *Jesus' love means that Becky's death is not the final word about Becky.*

I'm sure you understand some of these things better than I do. All that I have experienced about Jesus teaches me to trust God with all the hard-to-understand realities about suffering and death.

Thank you for listening. Thank you so much for sharing a piece of your life. You have really made a contribution to my life.

Sincerely,

Randy

ESTHER: *What to Do at Midnight*

Dear Randy,

Four years ago, after a tragic auto accident, I suffered a brain injury and lost my voice for over a year. Through many tests, my doctor told me about cancer.

I spent many months in the hospital experiencing all kinds of feelings and depression. I had a burning pain in my head for two years, along with a fever that wouldn't subside. My one ear grew shut and the bones in my chest became enlarged. I had bone scans and my doctor listed the name of "carcinoma of the bones." But I must tell you how God works miracles.

The doctor has told me that he feels I am fighting a losing battle because of the swelling of the liver and the toxins which accumulate too fast in the blood-stream. But I'm keeping my eyes on Jesus and thank Him that our battle is never lost with the Lord on our side.

I am under extremely heavy stress and need your prayers so much since I just recently lost my husband and three other members of my family in six months. At times I cry to God, "I can't go on, Lord." And He says to me, "How often would I gather you under my wings."

I am very much alone, as far as family or friends, because of handicaps; but really never alone with a God who cares. Your material was such a real blessing to me that I had to cry. I sit up at night to rest because of my heart, and when I can't sleep, I pray for all the suffering and afflicted.

In His love,
Thank you, with caring,

Esther
Indiana

What do we do when the bottom falls out? Sometimes coping is not enough. Esther must cling boldly to the fact that God loves her. I'm sure Satan whispers, "God does not love you. He has left you to stand alone." But she repeats the words of God to Jeremiah, "I have loved you with an everlasting love; therefore, I have continued my faithfulness to you." One of the unhappy secrets of the Christian life is that we're not promised deliverance from disaster. We are promised a way *through* the storm, not around it. Esther works hard to hold fast to three certainties:

1. God knows what is happening to me.
2. God cares about me.
3. God demonstrates His care by surrounding me with His love.

Although the psalmist didn't know *how* or *when*, he knew *that* "God will send from heaven and save me, He will put to shame those who trample me. God will send forth His steadfast love and His faithfulness." Esther knows this, too. She knows she can "cast all (her) anxieties on Him, for He cares about (her)." God knows the depth of our despair. John the apostle says God's love for us "was made manifest among us in His Son . . . that we might live through Him." Esther underscores rule #1 for sufferers who believe: *Cling boldly to the fact that God loves you.*

But there is a second rule closely related to the first:

Be sure to sing at midnight and pray for others. In the hours of the night, fears tend to enlarge and anxiety can run wild. In order to deal effectively with doubts, sufferers have to know what to do at midnight. Perhaps taking a cue from Paul and Silas, who sat chained in prison after a beating, we can pray and sing hymns to God. They certainly understood the darkness that comes from heavy stress, just like Esther. They exercised what Victor Frankl called the last great freedom—the freedom *to choose* how to react to horrible circumstances. They chose to praise God and pray.

Esther has the song of God's love in her heart, choosing to pray for the suffering and afflicted rather than dwell on her situation. How easy it is for me to be bitter and defeated, brooding about my losses. Not Esther. She numbers God's blessings. Instead of being overtaken by bitterness and despair, she has peace, and calm trust. She keeps her eyes on Jesus. She can sing at midnight. The psalmist declared:

> I waited patiently for the Lord, He inclined to me and heard my cry. He drew me up from the desolate pit, out of the miry bog, and set my feet upon a rock, making my steps secure. He put a new song in my mouth, a song of praise to our God (Psalm 40:1-3).

KATHY: *No Room for Self-Pity*

Howdy!

I have gone through 20 major surgeries in 14 years, three in the last ten months. Five of these were to remove tumors in early cancer stages (three in and around my right eye). In May of 1982 I was diagnosed as having Severe Intractable Menieres Disease Syndrome.

This is a disease with no known cure. It destroys the hearing and balance nerves. I suffer from severe attacks of dizziness, vomiting—pressure in the head and ear pain—loss of balance and hearing. I can't sit, stand, walk, or move without a lot of help.

The attacks come with no warning and last anywhere from a few minutes to hours or days. One of the worst attacks I had lasted six weeks. I can't be alone. I've had attacks that caused me to fall through a glass window and be cut real bad.

I recently went through training and received "Yosemite," a poodle trained to perform 100 tasks for me from retrieving the phone to turning lights on and off. He also gets help. But most important, having Yosemite allows me to be *alone!* I love to read, write letters, and be alone to think.

Now let me tell you about Walter—my husband— the father of our boys. Walter will be 39 on March 18. This man has given up all material things that most men believe to be symbols of success just so he could provide the necessities for us.

With all this we have had social workers and counselors tell Walter to walk off and leave us! He looks at them and says that's not an option. We married for better or worse, in sickness and in health! Walter seldom complains. When I touch his hand I feel such strength!

I've often wondered if things were reversed and he was ill instead of me if I would be able to care for him and the boys with such grace and understanding. We have had to sell our wedding rings in order to keep the heat in our home.

He has had to take a medical leave of absence without pay several times to care for me because we couldn't pay for outside help and I had to be cared for. Because my illness has lasted so long and is here to stay, people get tired of helping—or maybe they are overwhelmed and just can't cope with our situation on top of their own.

The church has helped by providing the evening meal since my arrival home from the hospital. When they can, they help with transportation to the doctor. They provided Christmas for the boys and have helped with food three or four times.

Our needs are so great that what is needed and what can be provided are far apart. However, we manage surprisingly well! We have struggled to continue to believe through our ongoing crisis. We have learned so much and have been able to help so many.

At some time or other we have had to go to all the social service agencies—so we now know what service they will provide and we have a personal relationship with the people who run them.

Until I became ill, Walter used to say that I wanted everything done yesterday! This is no longer true. I can't move fast now. For slowing our lives down and allowing—no forcing—us to enjoy each other, minute by minute, we praise God!

I really feel you can help us gain a greater insight into surviving a crisis and being able to keep God as number one in our life! Let me know if I've dumped too much on you. I do hope you don't mind my sharing our story with you. Thank you so much for *"caring."* Psalm 138:8.

In Christ,

Kathy
North Carolina

It's normal for suffering people to feel sorry for themselves—at least occasionally. It's hard to do otherwise. I encourage those in health crisis or those who have suffered significant loss to refrain from being too hard on themselves for thinking "poor me" at times. When I talked to Kathy on the telephone, I was impressed with her attitude. In our visit she stated matter-of-factly that she would be totally deaf and unable to talk to me by phone in a matter of months.

How, then, can she praise God? What can we learn about self-pity from those who suffer? Kathy certainly makes a strong case that there's no room for it. A friend of mine says there is no future in self-pity. The reason he gives is that the person who spends much time feeling sorry for himself concentrates on what he does *not* have rather than on what he has. He chooses to think about *losses* and the words *why, can't,* and *never again.* Hope and joy vanish from his vocabulary.

Another friend, a prominent psychologist who has had a bout with cancer, says what we don't realize is that *self-pity is often a result of choice.* He says when we (1) think mostly about *our* loss, (2) classify our situation as worse than most, (3) refuse to see any prospect of something positive in the situation, (4) say that we have no choice how we feel about it, (5) require that others tell us how awful our situation is, and (6) refuse to think about the needs of other sufferers, *we are making self-pity a choice.*

I'll never forget Kathy. She could fill the lead role in the play "The Unsinkable Molly Brown." She says to us, "Look, I know the reality of what has happened to me. This is the way it's going to be. I could dwell on the minus side or the plus side. I choose, because of who my God is, to dwell on the plus side." Kathy is getting on with living life as God's gift, filled with challenges and wonder. Sure, she gets discouraged. Yes, she has her moments of self-preoccupation. "Why me" crosses her mind. She says, "I have my bad days but never two in a row." She demonstrates the power of acceptance: accepting what has come in the light of the love of God. She's chosen faith over despair. She believes praise, not bitterness, is appropriate. I want to follow her example.

JIM: *Suffering Can't Be Compared*

Dear Randy,

At close distance I have seen my father resign the fight and go down in defeat. And I have even myself struggled against the power of despair and the utter hopelessness that can increase day by day.

Sadly, my father lacked the resources to resist. He did not know Jesus—and so he could not hope in the life with the Father. My situation was different. For one, my "disease" was not terminal, although at times I thought it must be, and other times I feared it might not be. It seems to me, though, that there are profound similarities between my father's disability and mine. He was in constant, unrelenting pain from his disease. I was in constant, unrelenting pain from a broken, shattered heart and terribly wounded pride.

I sought release in many worldly ways and I shook my fist at God for standing quietly by while the substance of my life was squeezed from me like the squeezing of the insides from a grape. I was angry because the heart of my life was gone. I despaired because the taking was permanent. But as I railed, and hated, and cried, and wept with the power of purpose, His voice came to me—not audibly, but quietly, incessantly.

"Peace, be still, and know that I am God." "No!" I cried. "I hurt, I won't be still!" But I was, finally. And I accepted, finally, who I was, what I was, and where I was. And I learned the meaning of "He who loves his life will lose it." And I wished with sorrow that I had learned before my father died so I could tell him.

There is faith, hope, and love. And to counter these Satan sends the circle of unbelief, despair, and hate. The circle is self-perpetuating and can be entered at any point. Beware in your pain and your sorrow—in your sense of loss. These are not blind platitudes we tell the world. These are words of power, and hope, and life.

With love, your brother in Christ,

Jim
Texas

When we compare our suffering with another person's, we are making a mistake. Suffering can't be compared. "Therefore we do not lose heart. Though outwardly we are wasting away, yet inwardly we are being renewed day by day. For our light and momentary troubles are achieving for us an eternal glory that far outweighs them all. So we fix our eyes not on what is seen, but on what is unseen. For what is seen is temporary, but what is unseen is eternal" (2 Corinthians 4:16-18).

Suffering is intensely personal and painful. Whether it comes from a life-threatening illness or a painful divorce, there's folly in thinking, "Well, he doesn't hurt like I do." I'm not suggesting that Jim's careful thinking about the similarities and differences between his father's situation and his own is a mistake. In fact, I see the possibilities for growth in his comments.

Dr. Alla Bozarth-Campbell writes of the common ingredients in successfully coping with all kinds of loss. Most sufferers, he says, experience the *shock*, then the *confusion*, followed by the *range of emotions*, then finally arrive at *ways to cope*. Finally, he is saying, you must have a plan of "what you're going to do about it."

Jim starts with the necessity of faith in Jesus Christ. This helps us to cope successfully. Just as Job's story demonstrates, both God and Satan have their agenda in the arena of human suffering. God's purposes, as Jesus made clear, are loving. Satan's purposes, always consistent with his nature, are to alienate us from God, destroying our trust in Him. We must beware.

GLENN: *A Perspective on What Really Matters*

Dear Randy,

The surgeon came into the waiting room and informed me my wife has terminal cancer. "How long," I ask. He said about two months. Then the shock wave hit me, a feeling of sadness, hurt, and anger came over me. I ask in silence, "Why my dear wife, why us, and why me?" The entire world seemed to be crashing in on me. My wife and I just retired recently. We had so many plans, doing things to make our house a good home and working in the yard. The doctor informed me I could bring my wife home.

At home our thoughts and values began to change. Materialistic things and plans that we considered of great importance had little meaning. Time became the greatest value. Every day, every hour, and every minute became so precious to us. As time passed I would see her in pain and her body deteriorating daily. This became a time of true testing of my faith in God. Even though I know the Lord Jesus, I would ask in my finite mind, "Why, dear Lord, are you taking her away?"

But God's will was being done. Our Lord has revealed, "It is appointed unto man once to die, but beyond the grave is the greatest hope. God gave His only Son to die on the cross that we may have eternal life. God will wipe away all tears and sorrow; sin, and death will be no more." How precious these promises became as my wife and I shared the few remaining days and hours together.

In the final hours after she lost consciousness I would hold her hand and continue to tell her of God's love and my love for her. I thank the Lord for the time He gave us to rededicate our lives to Him in her final hours.

Glenn
California

This letter was written after the acute grief had subsided and Glenn looked back at his loss within his Christian perspective. He had accepted the fact of his wife's death. He thought of his life with her in her last two months as precious time—time given to them by a loving God. He was able to share precious memories with his wife; he probably took several occasions to tell her how much he loved and appreciated her.

His letter reminds us that "life is a vapor" and that we can live wisely only if we are living with proper priorities, especially in our most important relationships. Sufferers consistently urge us not to take relationships for granted. They plead for persons to love one another every day. Glenn also speaks a word about the insignificance of material possessions. Suffering always sharpens our perspective on what's really important in life.

JIM AND BETH: *No One Seems to Care*

Dear Randy,

I am always encouraged after we talk. We got the report back from Beth's tests and things look good. The small mass—one in each of the lungs—is completely gone; the large mass in the chest cavity is 75-80% gone. The doctors think that the residual may be scar tissue. Now that the chemo is over, she is going to take radiation therapy for about four weeks, primarily for "insurance." We praise God for this good news!

The roots of our feelings during Beth's illness started over 15 years ago. My construction company failed at this time and we lost virtually everything we had (except the equity in our house). The horrible trauma that accompanied such an event almost crushed us. During this period, our oldest daughter (thirteen years) ran away from home for three days. The police found her. We found out years later that she has a congenital chemical imbalance which causes her to be emotionally unstable. She also has the symptoms of a manic depressive. She is doing much better now, but she will probably be under the care of a psychiatrist, occasionally, for all her life.

About five years ago, I had an artery collapse in my neck. For several weeks I had expressive aphasia. I could not read, write, nor speak in complete sentences. The doctor could not operate due to its location. Eventually, I regained over 95% of my processes. There was no medically explainable reason for the collapse.

When Beth was diagnosed as having Hodgkin's Disease a year ago, I felt like my world that had started to collapse 15 years ago was now going to collapse completely. The problems I had before were insignificant in relation to this one. We always felt like we could overcome anything as long as we had each other. It took several months for us to admit that she really had cancer. I took her to all of her chemo treatments and every time I went I'd see the sign "Cancer Center" and think, "We really don't belong here," or "Other people have cancer; we have Hodgkin's Disease."

Things rocked along pretty well until she started having chills and fever. The doctors made all kinds of tests but could not find out what was causing it. Several weeks later they finally determined that the catheter was infected. Minor surgery and antibiotics solved the problems. These days were the worst of our lives. It finally dawned on both of us that she could die of this disease. These were the days when we were so lonely.

It was during this period of time when not a single person from church came to see us or called. Her closest friend went three weeks without even touching base—the same friend that went by our house six, yes six, times a day. Another friend went by once or twice a day but never stopped or called. It was long past this time that some of my friends (two, to be accurate) asked me how I was doing.

It was during this time when Beth and I began to think back over the past few months and recount our contacts from our friends at church. It was then that we realized that not a single minister (we had three) nor their wives had stopped by to see her or us, nor had they called since she came home from the hospital (five months). The same was true for the elders and their wives. On occasion, when Beth was feeling okay, we would invite some friends over for snacks or even dinner, or we would go out to eat with them. Since her white count was always so low, she could not go to worship very often and when she did she had to avoid crowds; consequently, these were very lonely days for both of us.

We both became very angry. We finally realized that we didn't have many real friends. One couple at church and one lady in town were lifesavers. The couple (no children, both professionals) sort of adopted us and our condition. Although they lived in another town and were normally here only on Sunday, they would send little things, a card, a flower, all through our ordeal. Obviously, we became very close. The lady in town heard of Beth's disease from a newspaper article, came and introduced herself and came back practically every week. She was always bringing little things to Beth.

I continued to serve in the church during this ordeal, although not very well. I suppose that my resentment colored my attitude. I recall thinking that, if Beth were to die, I would not have anyone to conduct the funeral and wasn't sure who I would use for pallbearers! It makes me ill to think about it now. After all, our old Christian friends have also abandoned us. None of them ever called after first contact. Even today, we have not heard a word from most of these "old friends." We assume that they have heard from someone that Beth is still alive. We feel like calling and saying, "Hey, in case you're interested, we're okay."

In Christian love,

Jim
Nevada

We can't escape anger when we feel abandoned by people whom we have counted on to care for us during our time of suffering. Coping with the reactions of others is, sometimes a big task. We have expectations, especially of loved ones and friends. We are easily disappointed, even crushed, when they fail to provide the understanding and support that we need. It helps us to keep in mind that our loved ones and friends feel helpless also. They may fear that the patient will die. They may be upset with the situation in much the same way the sufferer is.

Sufferers often feel *isolated*. It's easy for them to wonder: Does anybody really care whether I live or die? When sufferers see a little evidence that someone has forgotten them, it serves as a megaphone to shout to their hearts what they most fear—"We are being abandoned and left alone in all this." Fear, their own fear, magnifies any inattentiveness into a major crisis.

What can help? Sufferers can help by cautioning themselves against jumping to the conclusion, "Nobody cares about me." It's a subtle form of self-pity and may not be true at all. Comforters can help by realizing this tendency and putting forth extra effort to show interest and concern. Christian comforters in the same church must realize that Jesus taught us to weep with those who weep and that Christian compassion is never feeling sorry for someone but acting to meet needs.

Sufferers feel isolated because, in some sense, they really are. They often have to curtail their normal activities. They are dealing with some level of fear and the denial of death. Necessary adjustments occur in relationships on the job and in the community. We should also keep in mind the difficulty all of us have in giving and receiving help. Typically, we have some difficulty in giving but maybe more in receiving.

It's not surprising that even some old friends stay away when a sufferer looks weak or sick. They may think, "He has too much company" or "she needs to rest." While sufferers may, as in this case, feel a strong need for contact, they will need to make that known clearly. I'm aware that the words *cancer patient* carry a stigma in some circles, causing discomfort to some. Loved ones and friends should work hard to overcome whatever stigma is felt, but the patient and her spouse must also work to relieve feelings of anger and frustration that their needs are not being met. It's a two-way street.

Since cancer patients can serve as unwelcome reminders of our own humanness and mortality, we must work hard not to avoid them during their illness.

Let me say a word about anger and resentment. Jim and his wife honestly express what they feel. They really don't like feeling that way. However, I would be upset, too. Their anger is the chief response to their greatest fear—rejection. Duncan Buchanon says that to be treated as a nobody is the worst insult of all. This is what we all tend to fear the most because there is in some of us a feeling that we are nobodies anyway.

Sometimes we think good or ill of ourselves based on who is paying attention to us. We can't wish our anger away and time doesn't always help. When we suppress it, we get depressed and this can lead to a paralysis. Some people who have felt overlooked describe their hearts as "a dam waiting to burst inside me." Anger can so burn that it saps the energy, leaving us exhausted and feeling sorry for ourselves. In every case anger must be dealt with in a healthy fashion before we can overcome it.

One possibility for Jim and Beth is to call a couple of old friends and say, "I'm feeling that we've kinda been abandoned." Another might be taking a friend to lunch and saying, "I'm upset that several haven't called or come by. Could you spend a little time with us? We're feeling left out." Forgiveness for those who have hurt us through inattention is essential. It's essential for *our* spiritual health. We may need to pray, "Father, forgive them, for they know not what they do," in the face of rejection, even unintentional rejection.

The best way is still for Jim and Beth to talk to the people. They will want to do better when they know what the needs really are. Sensitivity is sometimes a matter of training. Sufferers teach us to reach out to them by making us aware of the problem of isolation and feeling out of touch. Of course, we need them to be gentle with us when we fail to see their real needs.

ANN: *One Day Terminal Becomes Eternal*

Dear Randy,

As I am writing I am in very bad pain. I feel like Job in the Bible . . . and can say . . . though God doesn't answer my prayer for healing—still I love Him and trust Him.

My pain pills are not working now, and it is so difficult. There's not a thing I can do. If all the prayers from my wonderful friends could heal me, I would be up and running around the block, but nothing seems to help. I don't know the answer.

The chemotherapy has ruined all my nerve endings—thus the "tingle" all over the arms, legs, and back. I wouldn't wish my pain on any person. Only God knows the road ahead for me. I am ready to be with the Lord; suffering is too hard. I'm sorry to unload on all of you, but maybe you can understand a little of how I feel.

He must want to train us, even in this pain, to see if we can resist the devil and not deny Him. Perhaps He wants to test us to see if we can be trusted to choose Him. I know there is nothing we can do to earn heaven. Our Savior has paid the price already.

It is the fear of the unknown and I know that God tells us in the Bible hundreds of ways to trust and believe—and *our human ways* are weak. I am one of the weak. I have always been sheltered by a good husband. I've never been toughened by worldly knocks. Sometimes people that are can take things better.

I have always thought I could take any problems and I really have been able to trust God for everything—

but pain, terrible sickness, and death are the hardest things I have ever had to face.

I am pouring out my thoughts to you. Thank you for your concern.

Your friend in Christ,

Ann

———

Ann is terminal. She is sure, but doesn't know for sure. She has tumors in her liver. Every time she eats she gets deathly sick. It is so sad. I can hardly take it.

John (her husband)
California

What a moving letter! Perhaps this letter is one of the last ones Ann will write. Many emotions are stirred by the things she says. This sufferer is walking by faith, not sight—even at this difficult time. She doesn't fully understand everything, but she does know whom she loves and trusts. She is handling her suffering very well. This encourages me.

What is happening to Ann makes you despise the devil more and more. Decay, pain, and death are his work. He seems to be in the corner of the hospital room, glancing over at the person in the bed, laughing—enjoying the misery he has caused. But he will not laugh last. He will eternally wail in defeat, for he has been defeated.

Let's remind ourselves of what Ann still believes as she suffers: Jesus has solved the problem of sin, suffering, and death. (1) He came and suffered *with* us. (2) He transformed the meaning of our suffering—it is now part of his work of redemption, according to

Romans 8:19-25. As Peter Kreeft says in his excellent *Making Sense Out Of Suffering*, "Our death pangs become birth pangs for heaven, not only for ourselves but also for those we love."[6] Death is therefore not an end, but an entrance. (3) He rose victorious over death. This makes all the difference because our tears are not hopeless, but tears of joy that Christ has conquered our enemy. Paul can therefore say that our "momentary affliction," this earth's suffering, will be replaced by "eternal glory" (2 Corinthians 4:16-18). Therefore, there is really only one lasting tragedy possible in human life—not to be a Christian.

Another thought in Ann's letter deserves comment. John, her husband, says she is terminal. People often ask me to speak on "ministering to the terminally ill." It's a difficult topic. In part, the difficulty is in the fact that "terminal" can mean different things. It can mean, "She's dying now and I want to serve her," or "She's dying and she doesn't know it," or "She's dying and there must be something we can do." Ann needs reassurance from those who are already close to her— her family. Our service must address itself primarily to the family's needs.

Elizabeth Koop's book *Encounter With Terminal Illness* cautions us against treating the dying in a super serious manner, because we don't usually know when a person will die from an illness. We should leave the when to the doctors and God and concentrate our labor on the simple, tangible acts of kindness and service.[7] John's comfort and encouragement will be the first concern of those who are just now entering this situation wanting to know what they can do.

Hospital chaplain Dennis Saylor says that everyone in the family where a member is going to die deals with three things: (1) Anticipating grief, (2) dealing with the unresolved issues in their relationship and (3) dealing with spiritual anxiety.[8] The message of the gospel that death, though a final loss, is not the final story must be the supportive words to the family. Each of them must accept death as genuine loss while at the same time view death as ultimate gain, because of our faith in Christ. Saylor reminds us this is "a delicate balance for Christians. We don't grieve as those who have no hope."

Dr. Elizabeth Kubler-Ross' book *Death And Dying* is helpful in describing five stages through which dying persons generally go.[9] But we must be cautioned not to make too much of the stages because we can use what she's observed in ways that fail to bless and encourage those in the family who are going through the experience.

ANITA: *God Is Teaching Me*

To my big brother, Randy,

Right now I am at the University Med Center and in the a.m. I am going to have an exploratory lap and splenectomy. The Lord is caring for me and I stand awed at the way He consistently provides for my needs (when I let Him). I just want to be a light for Him—in life or death I want my purpose to be glorifying the Father of lights.

God takes such good care of me—even when my rebellious spirit (the natural man) doesn't want to accept His gifts. God is teaching my independent and willful heart to receive (such a beautiful lesson).

I'm so thankful that God has used this struggle with cancer to teach me of His abiding love and continual care. Even when, in my frustration, I push Him back and turn away, he is there just waiting to express a new form of His love.

Sometimes I just want to shout—"I'm not special just because I have cancer!" Maybe my attitude is wrong and I don't want it to be, *but* I get *so* tired of being treated special.

I can truly say I'm thankful for the last couple of years because the Lord has taught me lessons I hadn't paid attention to before and I feel closer to the heart of my Father. In a sense, I can say I've opened the box I kept God in and now I find He can't be contained in a box or by the limits of my imagination.

I just found out I will need six more months of chemotherapy. My spleen was tumor-free, but one of the lymph nodes they took was involved. I go in for the fistula—a vascular access—the 26th and will start chemotherapy two weeks later. I'm not sure how I feel; I'm just trying to be grateful. God thinks I can do it. I just want to trust.

Anita
Oregon

All of my correspondence with Anita deals with her pointing out lessons she is learning through her suffering. "I'm learning to lean on Him," "God is using my struggle," "the Lord has taught me lessons." When I first met Anita she was working in a hospital as a nurse, caring for others. Conscientious, attentive to detail, always willing to work double shifts, she was the kind of nurse anyone would want to have. She had a different view of herself. Her words included "self-centered," "shallow," "weak in faith."

She exhibits an improving self-image and a calm trust in God more now than when she first became ill. One reason is a friend who has spent hours reading Scripture with her and serving her needs during the hospital stays. Anita has learned that what she describes as "stubbornness" can be a beautiful trait of commitment to excellence in caring for others so that God will be glorified. She's a quality nurse. She feels that her suffering has refined her faith and given her a clearer picture of God. She thanks God daily for what He has taught her through suffering. I join her in giving God gratitude for His good work in her life. It sounds unusual to hear someone thank God for their suffering experience; but in Anita's case I understand and thank God, too.

Maybe Anita has a maturity in Christ that each of us needs. Peter says, "Count it all joy . . . when you have trials" because God is making your faith what it should be.

BARBARA: *Going Through It with Another*

Dear Randy and caring friends,

It's very sad that many of us never realize that we are so far "off course," until we find ourselves at one of life's crossroads or at an apparent dead end. If only we could all learn to view life as though it will soon be gone, we would surely be able to find more meaningful joy and do more of God's work for others. But often it takes a crisis to open our eyes!

My life had been progressing along, with the usual ups and downs and minor stresses and frustrations. I clearly remember, however, the sheer panic I felt when early last fall my dad and I first learned my mother had cancer. The thought was more than I could bear. Did she have only weeks to live, as was the case with her two older sisters? Or would she linger on, wither away, and endure the kind of suffering that my nearly 90-year-old cancer-ridden grandmother was experiencing? I was distraught with fear, grief, and worry.

Yet, from that very first moment, my mother demonstrated an inner strength beyond my wildest imagination. She had always preached to us that we should take one day at a time. Now, in the face of her crisis, she was determined to demonstrate her belief. Ironically, my mother's fight had just begun.

Throughout the past months, Mom received the majority of her chemo on an outpatient basis. Naturally, she had many days filled with violent vomiting and nausea, and experienced many of the countless side-effects that the drugs cause. Still, her spirits remained high, and her determination to fight helped her force down the necessary well-balanced foods (shortly after the preceding meal had come up!) After 11 series, she had received the maximum amounts allowed. The next step was more testing, to evaluate what progress the chemotherapy had brought.

Yesterday, my mother met with her doctor to learn the test results. What a wonderful relief—WHAT A JOYOUS FEELING—to learn her cancer is no longer visible! Praise the Lord! Of course, we know she has no fool-proof guarantee for the future. But I think we have all learned so much from this whole ordeal. None of us knows what our future days on earth hold. We must just trust God, and be appreciative of this wondrous gift of life we have—as well as the gift meanings, but especially two little drugstore plaques express it well for me. They read:

> Life is made up of little bits of time
> and each is a gift
> for us to love and cherish.

> What you are is God's gift to you—
> What you make of yourself is your
> gift to God.

God be with you and yours.

Sincerely,

Barbara
Michigan

Milton Meyerhoff wrote a small book entitled *On Caring*. He said: "To care for another person, I must be able to understand him and his world as if I were inside it. I must be able to see, as it were, with his eyes what his world is like to him . . . I must go into his world in order to sense from the inside what life is like for him. In caring, my being *with* the other person is bound up with being *for* him as well."[10]

When we are trying to care, we're always trying to understand what it's like for the other person to be going through his experience. Christians learn to do this by studying Jesus' life. Jesus took on human form and experienced what humans go through. He came on the inside. He didn't just say, "If I were you, I'd do this." He actually went through being human.

Barbara was a real encouragement to her mother because she hung in there with her, staying by her in down times and up times. Dietrick Bonhoeffer says in *Life Together* that each of us really needs someone to give us encouragement in times of despair and hope in times when everything seems hopeless. He says we need someone whose presence and message to us is a witness of the "Living Word."[11] Again and again when we become discouraged and uncertain of whose we are, we need someone to point the way for us. This accomplishes good results because, as Bonhoeffer put it, "the Christ in our hearts is weaker than the Christ in the Word of our brother; his own heart is uncertain, his brother's is sure."

When I was struggling with illness in 1981—my second battle with cancer—a beloved brother in Christ came time and time again and sat with me with words of reassurance about Christ. My own weakness left me vulnerable to doubts about God's care, but this brother regularly spoke a certain word, helping my heart to remain calmly assured. Hope and encouragement come from the Word. But sometimes the Word comes through a messenger. You can be that messenger for a sufferer.

ALICE: *A Breaking Point*

Dear friend in Jesus,

I need help making a decision. I am a past-81-years-old lady who is very ill with an abdomen that is in constant pain. After all kinds of tests and even surgery, the only diagnosis the doctors can come up with is a "spastic colon." They can do nothing for me—no pain pills. Besides that, I have a ventricular fibrildion of the heart which makes me so weak and dizzy that, except for going to the dining room for breakfast and lunch, I spend all the rest of my time lying down. I also have a very difficult time sleeping, never more than three or four hours a night. Life has become intolerable.

Before I get into suicide, though, I want you to know that I've been a Christian since I was 37. I was left alone then with two little boys, seven and nine. God led us to a small church where the children memorized one verse of Scripture a week. So I entered in also and from hearing each other say his verse, we all memorized all three. I am glad to state that we still know them all.

After being left alone, I entered U.C.L.A. and in 1941 graduated with a B.S. degree and a Ph.N. certificate, and that fall got a position as a school nurse in Los Angeles.

After retiring, I felt led of God to go to Mexico to work as a self-supporting volunteer missionary helper. I made eight round trips from Los Angeles to Guadalajara all by myself—in my little Corvair, which was packed solid with bedding, cooking utensils, dishes, etc. Nothing was ever furnished except the furniture. I had my own apartment, but was at the beck and call of any missionary to babysit, paint flannel backgrounds, and do upholstery, dress making, etc.

But three months into my fourth year there I got lombar pneumonia and coughed so much that my vocal chords were damaged. Now, I can't sing at all and my voice is so raspy.

I love Jesus beyond all else, but now I am so weak and ill I can't even go to church. Now, for the question: Do you think God would damn me to hell if I should take an overdose of sleeping pills some night and end it all (leaving no trace, of course, so my sons would never know)? I'm sure my M.D. would sign the death certificate "heart attack."

Please forgive the lengthy letter, poor spelling, and errors. I just wanted you to know that all my life, since I was 37, I have lived for Jesus.

Sincerely in Him,

Alice
California

Each sufferer has a breaking point. Each can take just so much. Sometimes it seems that if one more straw is added to our load, we will fall beneath it.

Don't overreact to the desire that some sufferers express to be through with it, to have it over. Before we reprimand, we must sit long enough to understand. Alice feels worthless at this point in life. She has lived a long, fruitful life, full of trust, and has served her Lord with a heart filled with love. She is in the later years of life and in very poor physical condition. Her pain is tearing at the quality of her days and deteriorating her will to live.

Of course, I pleaded with her not to take her own life. The real question in this letter went far beyond the one she asked. She wanted to be heard, understood, and cared about. In other settings, sufferers have asked me to pray with them that God would take them. Alice is ready to go, but she knows it is not a decision she should act upon. Sufferers sometimes reach points where they see no meaning and they want to go on and be with the Lord. However, believers who suffer are aware that their greatest goal is, "Thy will be done."

Trusting God's timetable is a task Alice will need help with.

FRANCIS: *When a Child Dies*

Dear Mr. Becton,

My youngest child died with cancer this year. We found she had cancer when she was 17. She had a rare type of muscle cancer. We went through all the possible types of treatment with her. She had 52 chemotherapy treatments, 28 radiation treatments, and two operations.

I cannot know just how much she really suffered; but as I was with her through everything, I know it is hard to watch someone you love very much suffer and not be able to take it away from them.

Betsy was a person with a strong faith and lots of courage. I know that faith is what upheld her and gave her strength to live while she was going through the winding down of her life. She touched many people's lives during her 21 months of illness. I myself received a lot of strength from her. It is not easy to give your child up, although I have four others. Still, each one has a place in your heart no other can fill.

Truly anyone who has cancer walks through fire. God was very merciful to my daughter. If she had lived much longer she would have been in much pain. He must have loved her a great deal to take her before the pain became unbearable.

I would like to be able to help others like her, for while she was alive there was not much time for me to do anything other than care for her. Though she is gone, I know there are many more like her.

Yours in Christ,

Francis
Mississippi

Notice the words of this mother, "It is not easy to give your child up." I can't begin to imagine how painful grief over your child would be! C. S. Lewis tells of losing his mother at the tender age of nine. Years later he wrote that with her death, "all settled happiness, all that was tranquil and reliable disappeared from my life." I can identify with that description because I lost my mother when she was 57 after she had been sick for seven years. But, to this date, I've not had to cope with the grief of burying one of my children (and I pray that I will not have this experience).

In 1981 the respected minister Dr. Wayne Oates wrote a book drawing upon his 40 years of caring for bereaved people and his own grief experience. The book, *Your Particular Grief,* is one I recommend to grieving people along with selected Scriptures. Dr. Oates understands grief and is a reliable guide to how grief heals. He points out that grieving takes different amounts of time for each of us. We first face the *shock* when we hear the news of the loss. As we absorb the shock we experience *numbness* and then a mixed *belief* and *disbelief* that this is really so. Then we have *depression* and *selective memory* when we seem to function well until something reminds us of our loss and it overwhelms us with fresh sorrow. Finally, some time later, we are able to turn back to life with a determined *commitment to rebuild* our lives.[12]

Sometimes it helps a person just to know that these phases he is going through are normal and can take as little as three months or as much as twenty months. Grieving happens to all of us, but it happens to us one at a time—uniquely and personally.

Believers, like Francis, often have spiritual struggles in their grief. Her daughter's death leaves her feeling powerless and weak. The psalmist says, "My heart aches, my strength fails me; and the joy of my life has gone from me" (Psalms 38:10). This should be recognized as a time when temptation to despair is near and Satan must be resisted. When the heart is full of deep sorrow, God can seem very far away and disinterested. But that's not true. This is a good time to pray that God, who is near, will give us His nearness to bolster our weakness with His strength. We must remember the promise of 1 Corinthians 10:13 that with the severe test comes "a way out" provided by God. God is able to strengthen perplexed people who lean on Him.

When the death of a daughter or son comes, we ask, "What's the meaning of this?" This cutting short of life seems to suggest to some that our lives are futile. But God comforts us and gives us new purpose and renewed meaning. Paul, in 2 Corinthians 1:3-4, suggests that God equips us through our pain to be a comfort to other hurting people. God saves us from the trap of self-centeredness and a "poor me" way of living by making us sensitive to others. This, of course, does not explain the nagging "why-did-this-happen" question, but it speaks to the question, "What do I do with this horrible experience?" Wasn't Jesus a minister to the brokenhearted? We are called to His ministry. Your personal grief can be used to show God's care to hurting people. That is exactly what Frances does, seeking to give God glory.

Why does a child have to die? Dr. John Claypool, in *Tracks Of A Fellow Struggler*—a powerful little book written about the death of a ten-year-old daughter—

tells of his anger and struggle with that question. He says, "There is more honest faith in an act of questioning than in the silent submission, for implicit in the very asking is the faith that some light can be given." Then he observes that we help grieving people not by trying to explain their tragedy. Evil and suffering, he says, are "deeply mysterious." He suggests that we grapple with our faith, making sure it is real, acknowledging that life is God's gift to us. "To be angry because a gift has been taken away is to miss the whole point of life . . . gratitude and humility rather than resentment should characterize our handling of life."[13]

Dr. Claypool's words may not comfort every grieving parent, but his *honesty* with his feelings about his own grief is encouraging. He says the one certainty is that God knows what He is doing and can be trusted with the great "unfairness" of life.

JAMES: *He's Doing "Just Fine"*

Brother Randy,

We lived in Syracuse, New York, when Mary found a small lump on her chest. Mary made an appointment to see a doctor, and he told her to wait a few weeks to see if it went away. It didn't. They decided to do exploratory surgery. By the time she came back from the operation they had removed her spleen and several lymph nodes. I was just then starting to worry.

The doctor told us it was cancer, Hodgkin's Disease. We both cried and did not know what to expect. We were scared to death because what we knew about cancer was very little, except that Mary was going to die. No matter what the doctor said, I could see no hope. We were both new Christians and had not learned all the things that we should have known or that we needed to know at that time.

I was scared to death—thinking mainly of myself, I guess. I had one boy at home who was ten years old and another boy who was three months old. A Christian woman had taken Tim, who was the baby, and kept him at her house for over a month while Mary was in the hospital. She would pick John up from school and take him to her house, would do all our laundry, and supplied us with supper at her house every night. They lived about 15 miles from us and she did this every day. I could not believe that a person whom we had known for just a few months could show this much caring for us.

All my family lived in Nebraska and Mary's family could have cared less. Both her parents were dead and she had eight brothers and seven sisters, but none offered to help. When told that Mary had cancer, I could not go to work that day. I went out to the car and spent an hour crying. I needed someone to share my burden with but I didn't know who would care. I went to our preacher and told him how I felt and I didn't think that he really understood. He felt that I was feeling sorry for myself. Maybe he was right, because I didn't know if I could handle it. I didn't think about if Mary could, just if I could. That's the first time I had ever cried around another person. I went away still not knowing what to do and not having the faith in God that I should. I never considered that He was going to take care of us. I thought I was going to do what needed to be done on my own, but I soon found out that was impossible.

Mary finally came home but had to go in five days a

week for four weeks for radiation treatment. Tim was now at home and Mary was so sick from the treatments. But every day that I left for work some lady from the church would be there to spend the day taking care of Tim and John and Mary. Every day Sue, the elder's wife, would take Mary to the hospital for treatment. Every day some ladies would bring our meals by. This went on for over three months.

I could not believe that people could care so much or would go out of their way to help us as much as they did. They had special prayer sessions at the church on Saturday mornings to pray for Mary, and I started to see God's love really working. I knew there was no way I could ever pay them back. I always paid my way, and now I was at a loss. Mary was now taking chemo treatments and after a few months things calmed down. But those Christians, whom I knew fairly well by now, were still there helping.

What really floored me was when Sue, the elder's wife, who had done more than any one lady should have to do, sent me a letter and thanked me for giving the church the opportunity to help us. I could not believe that she would thank me when we were the ones doing all the receiving. Sue told me that one thing the church had been lacking was "real love," and that we had helped everyone to find what this love was all about. No person can help but grow in that type of atmosphere—and grow we did. Nothing has helped us more through these years than our faith in God and fellow Christians. Mary was always so strong. Whenever or wherever she had the chance, she was sharing her faith and hope with someone around her.

We then moved to Nebraska and spent five years there before moving to El Paso. During this time Mary's cancer would go into remission and then flair up again. It seemed to be a never-ending battle. The biggest struggle that we had always seemed to be financial. Insurance never paid what we thought they should and it seemed like we could never catch up.

We had the hospital, doctor, pathology, and radiology offices calling us, "When were we going to send them more money?" They would usually call during the day when I was at work and talk in not too nice terms to Mary. When I came home she would be all upset and crying, saying she wasn't going back for any more treatments until they were paid. It seemed we were always under stress because of this. (If there are churches that can help those who have problems like this, keep encouraging them to seek out those they can help. I know the stress that a person can be under when all those bills start coming in. It's not a one-time deal like a lot of illnesses are. It's something that, many times, can go on and on for years.)

I know what Mary deserved on this earth and I wish that I could have given her more. But I also know the reward that she now has. In February Mary had some problems and they couldn't find the reason, so it was back to the hospital for tests. To me this was getting to be a habit that never seemed to stop. Oh, it felt so good that year and a half when Mary was in remission. We were able, during that time, to get most of the bills paid and to finally see our way out. Now this. Why? I love God. We served in any way we could. We had the opportunity finally to help some others out, and now here we go again. I hate to even say it, but I hated going to that hospital every night and saying, "Don't worry. Everything will be alright." Mary was telling me, "You deserve better than this," and "Think of all you could have if it wasn't for me." WHY GOD? WHY US AGAIN? WHY, GOD? But God gave us brothers and sisters who cared, and I thank Him for this.

And then the report. They had to do surgery to find out, but it was Hodgkin's again. After this they told her the type of chemo she would have to take. She said she wished she would just die and have it over with. I remember times when we had quarrels and Mary would say, "I wish that I would just die." And I would tell her that I really wished that I could, too. Sometimes I really felt that way, too. I wished that I would just die and have it all over with. Of course that would pass, but no one seemed to know just what I was feeling. I would always tell them that everything was fine, and still do.

I know that if someone is in the hospital or someone dies, a lot of people rush right over to offer their help, and bring food, and send flowers and cards. But after a week they seem to think that it's all over with.

After a few treatments, Mary told me that after all she had been through for all those years, she had never felt before that she was going to die. But now she did and she was scared. She told me many times how lonesome she was. She felt that the world was passing her by and that she was just sitting back and watching it pass. She told me that she wished I could feel the loneliness she felt, sitting at home every day and spending most of it in bed because she was too sick to get up. No one was coming to see her because they told me they thought she was too sick to want company and she needed her rest. I know now that if they would have done nothing but sit there, but at least been there, that's all it would have taken. But I knew that she had gotten better in the past and she would again; it just took time. BUT!!!

I was in the hospital with back problems when they brought Mary in because she was so sick. I had been in a week and they had me on some pills. I was alert, but forgot most of what was going on or what was said to me. I knew that Mary was in isolation and no one but the nurses had been able to go in for the last few days. But I never realized how bad she was. No one told me because they didn't want me to worry, or else they thought that I knew. (This is what I was told after Mary died.) Several wished that they had told me. They were keeping informed and had been in a few days before to see Mary. Now I hear, "I wish I had come and told you so you could have seen her." (I hadn't seen Mary for almost two weeks.) I never knew—OH, HOW I WISH I HAD— how lonesome she must have been in that room by herself.

What do I do now? I don't know? I know that the bills still come in—house payment, car payment, lights, water, insurance, plus now the final time for all the hospital and doctors for awhile, I hope. Oh, there's also the funeral home. I don't want to forget them. And John wants to go to college this fall. I never had any insurance on Mary because nobody would insure her, no savings because we never had anything left to save. I paid all the bills I could last week and have a total of $9.72 in my checking account and this next week's check is already gone.

School begins in about a week and a half and school supplies and clothes are needed for Tim. Car insurance is due this month. God, as you can see, I need to depend on you, because I see no way out. Maybe this is the way you meant it to be.

I've found out, finally after all these years, what loneliness is. Mary kept telling me, but I didn't understand until now. Oh, how I miss Mary. I knew I loved her, but I didn't realize how much. She could be in the hospital for a month, and yet I knew I could go see her. But now I can't; she's gone. And how I wish that the Lord would come, and come quickly, so that I could be with her again and not have all these things to worry about. God, I know I shouldn't worry . . . but I do.

I have been wanting to tell someone some of the things that I feel and now I've told you. I feel lots better.

God bless you brother,

James S.

I met James on a lovely spring day in a large university town. Camilla and I had been asked to hold a Caring workshop in the church where he is a member. I spoke to the men and Camilla taught the women. Then I gave the morning sermon on Compassionate Concern for the Sick. I remember the main emphasis in the sermon, based on the good Samaritan story in Luke, was that Christian compassion is not limited to a feeling; it is action on behalf of another. James and his children were there. After the sermon he came up to speak to me.

I had been told that James had just lost his wife, so I

knew his situation when he introduced himself to me. This soft-spoken, gentle soul looked tired. (Grief has a way of writing messages under the eyes.) I asked James what many others had probably asked him whenever they saw him, "How are you?" and he replied, "Just fine."

The words were right, but the tone was wrong. He wasn't "just fine." After the crowd thinned out a bit, I asked him to sit down and visit with me for a few minutes. As I listened to him talk about Mary's death and some of the problems *since* her passing, I realized that something unusual was happening. Those who had informed me about James and Mary had remarked about how strong he was spiritually, how well he was doing with her death and what a fine example of faithfulness he was. I saw something in him that no one had pointed out to me. Here was a broken and needy man. He was "putting up an appearance," saying, "I'm doing fine." But the people asking the question, the people who genuinely cared, weren't listening carefully to the answer.

In short, the situation was this: his fellow Christians thought James was doing fine and making it spiritually and financially, when in fact he wasn't making it at all! He was under strain physically, emotionally, financially, and spiritually. The communication reminded me of two people passing in the night, neither sensing the presence of the other. There were caring Christians and there was a needy man, but neither knew about the other.

I found out what the real situation was. I then asked James if he would write me a letter telling me about what he experienced and felt during Mary's illness and death. He wrote more than you have read. He opened the floodgate of his heart and eight years poured out. He wrote, "I have things on my heart that are so heavy that I want to tell someone—someone who will understand. But I don't know where to start or what to say." On the contrary, I think James knew where to start and what to say.

I don't share his letter to make anyone feel guilty. I share it as a representative letter of what many sufferers have told me. There is a chorus of voices who "want to tell someone how I really feel." There are numerous sufferers who try to give the impression that they're "doing just fine." Whose responsibility is it to meet these unmet, unspoken, needs? Yours, mine, and theirs. All of us are deficient in sensitivity, in hearing what a person is really feeling. And hurting people, for different reasons (including pride) sometimes fail to tell us how they really feel. Honest communication on the part of all concerned is what we need.

But there is more to James' story—more than even I know. I carefully sought to share with the church a truer picture of James' situation, and the response was heartwarming. They wanted to do more. Their desire to serve was genuine. God's people will "do better when they know better." What about you? There are probably many people like James in the congregation where you are.

BILLIE: *Equipped to Handle Fear*

Dear Randy,

I have ovarian cancer which I discovered last March. My tumor was at stage two. I had radiation and now I am taking chemotherapy. My drugs are cisplatnum and adreamician (I can't spell). I would like to know if you know of any other cases of ovarian cancer that have been treated with chemotherapy with success.

Any encouragement that you could send me on ovarian cancer will be deeply appreciated.

Sometimes I feel so alone and scared—fear, bitterness and despair just overwhelm me. My tests have all been negative, which I try to tell myself is a good sign. But fear of the disease and fear that the chemotherapy won't kill the remaining cancer cells is on my mind all the time. Fear that it will spread in spite of the drug is on my mind always.

Did you go through these fears? How did you learn to deal with them? I fear that success with ovarian cancer in the past has not been too bright. Please send me any information you can find that may encourage me.

I believe in God and life after, but at 34 years old I just can't seem to accept death and leaving my young family. The thought of death overwhelms me. I'm just not ready yet; that is why I look so hard for encouragement. Please let me know how other people feel on chemotherapy. Do they have muscle pain or bone pain, etc.? My leg has started aching for the last week and I worry. Did you ever think of suicide and not fighting any more?

My children also want to pretend I only have the flu and it will of course go away. I feel I am letting my husband down because I don't feel good enough to be as much of a companion to him as I used to be. He wants the same old cheerful, happy Billie again. And as hard as I try to be cheerful, I'm just not as carefree as I was. So I feel I am failing everybody. It is hard to *try* to live up to my family's expectations and as a result I feel guilty. I also worry about becoming very ill and being a burden to my family (heaven forbid). That is really my biggest fear, and it also causes guilt feelings. Nobody wants to do such things to their loved ones. God helps us; all we can do is try our best and hope and pray.

I was also very independent until I discovered my illness. What a shock! I have been stripped down layer by layer to my "inner self" also. But I have learned much of value in this last year about myself, my independence, and God. I also knew I couldn't face this on my own. I *really* needed God in my life. I am still struggling with a *whole lot* of fears every day. But I am facing it so much better now than in the first several months. I know it is because I turned to God and study His Word and pray for strength.

I am trying to look at one day at a time now. But it sure is hard. What a way to *have* to face life—a constant battle—when it should be with joy. But we have to accept things as they are, not as we wish they were. And with God's help we will continue to struggle on. I only pray that Jesus will be very close to all people with special problems.

I am happy that I have become close to God and I did it *because* of my illness and my need for Jesus in such a crisis. That is at least one great benefit out of this problem. I don't know the "why" of it. Maybe God has a purpose that we don't understand. Or maybe I am just a victim of circumstance. But we must believe that God loves us very much and has promised us a better life in the future. I must trust, love, and lean on Him even though I can't understand why I have this problem. Please write to me again. It feels good to share secret feelings with someone who cares and understands.

Sincerely,

Billie T.
California

Mary Beth Moster writes in *Living With Cancer* that each sufferer experiences negative emotions. But the real danger is that these negative emotions "can rule us and rob us of our joy."[14] Our fears—those painful feelings of large dangers about to come upon us—cause us to search for answers, to try to regain control. Believers who suffer know that God "has not given us the spirit of fear; but of power and love" (2 Timothy 1:7), but they sometimes are overwhelmed by fears. Sometimes the fear is so strong that we are even afraid of being afraid.

Some people respond to fear by withdrawing, getting depressed, and even becoming very demanding of others. Our fearfulness seems to be centered in anxiety about losing emotional control. When C. S. Lewis, in *A Grief Observed*, described his grief, he said, "No one ever told me that grief felt so much like fear." For him it was the same sensation—the nervous stomach, the unsure feeling, the restless spirit, the gripping "what ifs" that invade the mind.

Our words of reassurance that there is no need to fear do not necessarily erase the fears. These fears are strong, and they are ever-present. I encourage people to understand that these fears are natural and part of being human. We should not be ashamed or hesitate to express fear. God will come alongside our fearful heart and give us peace. He will remind us that we are His, regardless of the circumstances.

When we deal honestly and openly with our fears, some of them are not as "scary." What are you afraid of? "Death, you say? Or is it suffering a slow and difficult death? You're secure in God's love, but you don't want to leave small children right now? Of course, I understand. I wouldn't want to die right now either." If you were to say that to Billie, she likely would relax and breathe a sigh of relief. Her fear, if we can "normalize" it by understanding it, can be placed under her faith that God hears her when she talks to Him about it. He understands how strongly young mothers feel about such matters of the heart.

When life-threatening illness hits, the questions we have mostly deal with life, not death. Will I handle this well? Will there be enough money? What will the children do? What about the pain? Will my husband or wife stand by me in this? The uncertainties and anxieties are mostly about life. What then will help Billie the most? Information about her illness will be helpful. This will probably lessen her anxieties. Restatements of her faith in God as her loving Father, by herself and by those closest to her, will help. Thinking in daily segments, one day at a time, rather than a year or five years will help Billie.

Sharing information openly and honestly, refocusing one's faith, seeking to live one day at a time—these help keep fears manageable. Added to that, a fighting spirit, an interest in serving others, and a caring, supportive climate of friends and loved ones are allies in the fight against fears. For a few sufferers fear goes away; but for the largest number fear remains a constant battle. With Christ and God's tender spirit these fears can be beaten back. With each battle He gives the strength to overcome.

Remember too, fear of the unknown and the knowledge that we aren't in control of what happens allows us to lean on God rather than ourselves. Everyone comes to understand this reality, whether sufferer or non-sufferer. Suffering isn't the only arena of life where fear operates or dominates. If, in facing our fears, we realize our inadequacy and God's adequacy, then we have been served well.

Fear is largely based on what we do not know. Therefore, we must trust God, who desires only our good. I believe Billie experienced a release from the oppression of her fears. It came gradually through her decision to trust God and to be knowledgeable, open, and honest with her feelings. In this way God strengthened her ability to handle her fears.

I remember the young mother who wrote:

> My very soul is drenched in tears.
> My waking moments filled with
> Hopes slipping into fears.
> Sometimes it's peace and joy more than sorrow.
> Why can't I just accept now and let
> God take care of tomorrow?

TRUDY: *Dreams for the Future*

Dear Randy,

The first time I had cancer I was getting married in June and moving to Chicago. It didn't work out that way. I had an operation April 3, chemo April 11-15, and was married April 19, then four more rounds of chemo and an operation. All clear until May 1981; then it was back. My husband and I were planning to move to Phoenix. He was just about to give notice here in Tucson. I had my old teaching job back and it looked perfect.

I can't get over the guilt of what this disease did to my husband's career, twice. He is so supportive and wonderful. I'm also afraid to dream, to plan, to really get excited about the future that has cancer in it. Anytime I do a big change comes around.

I try to trust God. I trust Him eternally; I know He didn't give me cancer. I also know He could have kept it in check. I know healing is for His glory and I too believe in intercessary prayer.

I'm so contradictory—I want to live for my husband, because I love life and my family and fellowship with other ones in Christ. But what kind of life is one with cancer? I go in every time my blood count is good to be blasted with Cytoxin, Velblane and Bleomyacin, with no guarantees it's going to work. Who ultimately works is God.

I truly am in turmoil over my emotions on not really wanting to fight to live. My husband still can dream—I so want to and see these realized: children, a home (house type), ministering to others in a church—not always being ministered to. I also want him to be happy in a job with a future. In a nutshell this is how I feel.

Love through two bonds—our Lord and illness,

Trudy W.
Arizona

A large part of the joy in living is the joy of planning, dreaming, and working toward future goals. Trudy is now "afraid to dream." She contemplates a future "that has cancer in it." She has full confidence in the future, spiritually speaking, for her soul is healthy and her trust as a Christian is secure. She knows the future is as bright as the promises of God. But she faces life with a big question mark and a cloud of uncertainty over her health. She must trust God one day at a time, but what does this do to "planning?" It's hard to be seriously sick—harder than most of us think. She'll have to discipline her thinking about ways she can live her life without regard to her illness. She knows she is far more than a disease. But disease keeps her a bit off balance.

Trudy is riding an emotional roller-coaster. She can't fully trust her emotions. She lives with the knowledge that statistically she may not be a long-term survivor. How does that affect her? How would it affect you?

One of Trudy's needs is a supportive fellowship. Ideally, she should meet with fellow-sufferers from the cancer experience. One patient who started such a support group described the need for a "supportive fellowship" this way: "To have cancer is to have pain, discomfort, and the threat of death. It involves a loss of control over one's destiny. It is a permanent and unpredictable dimension in life that one must cope with. It is to be touched by the Almighty, but how that touch is felt, where the pressure is the heaviest, is very different for all . . . For those of us who are faced with life-threatening illness, there is a great need for a supportive fellowship group."

She then listed these objectives for such a fellowship:
1. To provide a release for fear, grief, depression, anxiety, anger, and loneliness.
2. To share experiences and problems, thus gaining emotional support, understanding, and acceptance from one another.
3. To convey hope, optimism, and encouragement.

4. To aid in adjustments to the situation and to promote understanding in the families.
5. To seek to live one day at a time.
6. To grow spiritually to the point where, if death comes, it may be faced with calmness.

Sufferers profit greatly from a supportive fellowship. Most understand their need to center around the *commonness* of their experience, thereby fighting isolation and loneliness. Also, the ability to care for others gives a dimension to one's own life—an expression of self-giving love. To care for others, living "beyond myself and my problems" brings joy, meaning, and satisfaction. A supportive small group may open up vital understanding of the illness and strengthen love for others.

MICHELE: *God Is in Control*

Randy,

You know how the Lord helps us grow through trials. Well . . . I got really sick. I had a bad kidney infection, started to get better, and got another infection. I almost lost my kidneys, had a temperature of 105 and had to go into the hospital. Right before I went to the hospital, the doctor did a pap smear. It came back abnormal and I had another one done. It also was abnormal—class III. So I went to a gynecologist. He did a clposcopy (that magnifies the area), then he had to do a biopsy. After the biopsy I hemorrhaged for ten days. The biopsy came back positive. I have cancer of the cervix. It's a little past the microinvasive stage. He did cryosurgery yesterday.

It takes two weeks to recover from that and I will

have to have a hysterectomy. Sometimes the cryosurgery buys extra time. He doubts that I can ever have children, because I have herpes (a virus which doubles the risk and may be a cause of cancer). That's the part that bothers me—not able to have kids.

You know, it's hard to face death statistics when they are your own. One thing I'm having trouble with is realizing that God is in everything. It's hard to believe cancer is from God. But God is in control. I do know that; it's hard to feel it though. But I'm sure this will help me deal better with my patients who have cancer. Because I can deal with patients who have knee surgery and with people who come from a horrible home life. So I guess this, too, will help me be a more effective nurse—for the patient's sake. I've seen so many nurses who are non-caring. I pray I never get that way.

Love in Christ,

Michele W.
Arkansas

It's difficult to be a young nurse, just having passed your state boards, and then to be told you have cancer. Michele is coping very well. One reason she does well is her conviction that God is in control. Leslie Weatherhead commented about "snap judgment" on God in the face of suffering: "I find comfort in the thought that I should be foolish to draw final conclusions when the purposefulness of God was only partially revealed. One doesn't walk through a theater and, from a few minutes' experience of the first act, make a deduction about the plot of the whole play or the character of the author. Yet, this is what we do about God."[15]

An unknown author has commented on the ancient art of rug-making while affirming that God is in control.

> My life is but a weaving
> Between my Lord and me;
> I cannot choose the colors—
> He works steadily.
>
> Often He weaves sorrow
> And I in foolish pride
> Forget He sees the upper
> And I the underside.
>
> Not till the loom is silent
> And the shuttle stops its fly
> Will God unroll the canvas
> And explain the reason why.
>
> The dark threads are as needed
> In the Weaver's skillful hand
> As the threads of gold and silver
> In the pattern He has planned.

The late Senate chaplain Peter Marshall liked to use the illustration of an oyster. He said the oyster could shake a fist in God's face and complain about the irritation and pain caused by grains of sand. But he would only show his ignorance of the process by which a lovely pearl was being formed. He affirmed that God's purpose with a human being holds the same mystery but also will end in the same beauty. While the purpose of God in one sufferer's experience is not always clear, the claim of believers is that He does have purpose. A puzzle it may be, and only a piece, at that. But all the pieces will fit together. Paul says that all things will be summed up in Christ. Everything will eventually find its place under the great purpose of God, which is to bring us to Himself through Jesus Christ (Colossians 1:20-22).

The essence of what Jesus said about God is that the whole world, both present and future, is under His Fatherly care and that Christians as His children participate in His victory over sin and death. All of this is according to God's plan and timetable. Jesus, in Luke 20:34-38, refers to "sons of the resurrection." According to the Scriptures, we know this victory is certain and guaranteed. That's why believers who suffer look at their experience as temporary. As Paul says, "The sufferings of this present time are not worth comparing with the glory that is to be revealed to us" (Romans 8:18).

Elton Trueblood affirms in *A Place To Stand*, "We cannot, if we believe in God at all, believe in His defeat."[16] He will triumph over the devil because He is sovereign Lord of His universe and He will accomplish His loving purpose. Divine justice wins. The problem of evil is finally solved. That's why Paul used the resurrection of Jesus to persuade listeners that God "has given assurance to all men" that He is in control by raising His son.

Michele reassures herself that "God is in control." For her and for us all, the message is reassuring. But it's reassuring precisely because it's true.

BELLE: *Profile of a Fighter*

Dear Randy,

My own sons, according to their doctors, were incurable. But thanks to the good Lord they are doing real well. James has been in and out of so many hospitals over the country. He's had so many operations. Only God could have pulled him through. He has been so close to death that everyone calls him God's miracle boy. Millions of prayers have been sent to God's throne for him.

I've heard him talk to the doctors and beg them, with tears flowing down his cheeks, not to let him die until he could see his daughter finish school and college. Only mothers can feel such hurt and seem so helpless. Prayer is to let God know we care— when only He can cure. They say James' cancer has had a remission. If only it will last.

Joe, my other son, has cancer of the liver. He has gone through untold pain and suffering. They cut into him and sewed him back up—told him he'd be dead in two months. That's been a year ago last August. He looks like he had never been sick.

My husband died with cancer. He was sick only two months, four days after he first saw a doctor. That will be 13 years ago. My youngest daughter, Julia, was 37 years, ten months old when she passed away. Of all my hurts this was the greatest blow I've ever had. She worked at a hospital for 14 years as assistant manager of the medical records and read and learned everything she could get her hands on. She knew all about her trouble and never told anyone. She had been with her father and two brothers in all their suffering.

I am 70 years old, live alone, and am crippled in my left ankle with osteomyelitis. Arthritis is in both upper arms, shoulders, and back. I have hypertension and diabetes—you name it. I try not to give in to any of them, but the last year or so has seemed to slow me down. But with Christ and God's help I'll make it. Continue to pray to God for Him to show me what He wants me to do. I'll keep trying.

Yours in Christian love,

Belle W.
Texas

Belle has been through it. I think of the book *When Life Tumbles In*. Belle is in pain. She lives with the loss of her daughter and her husband and the illness of her sons; yet she blesses God rather than cursing life. I want to know her better, don't you? She undoubtedly will make it to the finish line, "faithful until death." Her life has been characterized by a dogged determination to serve God, undeterred by her suffering. At age 70 she is still saying to God, "Here am I, send me. Show me what you want me to do. I'm ready." Don't you love her statement, "I'll keep trying"?

I want to use Belle to comment on what so many sufferers tell me about the importance of a fighting spirit. New research is demonstrating that "fighters" who refuse to give in to their disease can sometimes enhance their prospects for recovery. I'm inclined to believe that sufferers who fight against a "poor me", surrender-and-give-up view have the best chance to mature through their suffering. They do this by choosing to use their experience to (1) re-examine life's priorities, (2) refocus spiritually, and (3) use their suffering to bless others. It may be natural to turn inward when going through a suffering experience, but there is so much to be gained by turning upward (toward God) and outward (toward others). See if this is true for you. Make some sense out of your suffering.

We may feel hopeless and defeated, but if we belong to God we have tasted a hope and participated in a victory that has forever changed us. I believe it changes the way we look at life's losses. Jesus makes all suffering only temporary. As one writer says, "He defanged death," leaving it powerless. Believers participate in His work. Because of this they reject a "victim mentality." They also offer their suffering to God for His glory. Paul tells Christians they "participate in the sufferings of Christ." At least part of the meaning of this is that suffering experiences don't conquer those in Christ, whose Father is God. Rather, they are a part of His purpose.

I have heard doctors say that they prefer a patient of faith over one who has none simply because, generally speaking, their emotional tools to fight illness are better. Increasingly, researchers are showing the "linkage" between the beliefs and emotions of a person and the immune system. Those with a healthy faith (and many do not have a healthy faith) cope better with distress, dejection, and anxiety. Dr. Bernard Siegel, a surgeon from Yale's New Haven Hospital, researched the characteristics which "exceptional" patients exhibit. He found several but none more important than a healthy faith and a fighting spirit. There is increasing evidence that the right mental attitude helps the immune system function more effectively.

I am going beyond this physical realm to suggest that the right spiritual attitudes affect the health of the soul. I encourage sufferers to fight to find meaning in their suffering. Fight for a clearer vision of the God you love and trust. And yes, fight for your life, too, as long as you also say, "Nevertheless, not my will but Thine be done."

MRS. H. W.: *Alone in a "Couple World"*

I know what it is to be alone with no more goodnight kisses and arms around my neck. Heartbreak and sadness affects us all alike. Our only child, a son age 36, had Hodgkin's Disease for about four years. I know very well those months of suffering, those nightmares he went through with cobalt and chemotherapy, and finally death less than three years ago. My husband and I were heartbroken.

Then we discovered that my husband had advanced cancer of the liver. He died about six months after our son passed away. No one was in the hospital room with me to comfort me as I watched my Christian mate draw his last breath. I was not angry, nor frustrated, nor did I blame or question God. He was with me and gave me the strength I needed to continue in His service.

In less than four years I had lost my father, mother-in-law, father-in-law, son, and husband. I am living alone now in the country and drive 22 miles (one way) to worship—twice on the Lord's day and on Wednesday nights. I'm so thankful that all my family were Christians. Yes, our wonderful God and Savior is with His children and knows all about our sorrows and tears.

But the suffering is there, the realization that death is permanent, the one you lived with for over forty years is gone. No one understands you or knows how you think—the loneliness of widowhood, loneliness of decisions, not having anyone to discuss problems with, having the weight of making decisions. The full responsibility weighs heavily on a woman's shoulders already sagging with her own grief. Loneliness in worshipping alone; you return home feeling like you left something, a part of your worship, at the building. You become a fifth wheel. Our society is a *couple world,* so it seems you are excess baggage.

I guess I am now in the "recovery period." I'm still working on the period of adjustment. The Lord, our great physician, does care for us. Oh yes! *God cries with us!*

In Christian love,

Mrs. H. W.
Texas

I'm struck by the maturity of the woman who wrote this letter. One mark of this maturity is her acceptance of the inevitability of suffering without being reduced to a whimpering, paralyzed person. She has experienced pain and is honestly in touch with her feelings about her losses. But her response transcends despair. The time comes when everything we thought was nailed down comes loose—when people we thought would always be there turn out not to be. We long for a place where we don't have to say "good-bye," and we know this world is not that place.

Mrs. H. W. is growing through her grief experiences and adjusting with the grace that God supplies. It's still lonely, but she calmly trusts. How I would like to be like her. I wonder what made her that way. Isn't she a victim? Why does she sound like someone who intends to be victorious? She chooses trust in the silence of her pain. She grieves as someone who has hope. Her inner peace, I believe, is the result of a process and not a sudden occurrence. She has learned to deal with her sorrow, her loneliness, even her worries one step at a time.

She credits God for giving her the strength to go on and helping her reject bitterness. We must learn that real peace grows out of fellowship with God. People ask, "How do I prepare for life's losses?" Prepare your spirit first to praise God for all the gifts of life. Trust Him with each day's struggles, seeking not so much answers but a vision of how to respond in a trusting way. Hold on tightly to the Christ who died and was raised again.

As you practice these choices, reaffirming your decision that God is the center of your life, you will be living the abundant life which Christ supplies. This will mature your faith so that losses, even though painful and—for a period—paralyzing, will not be terminal to your faith. You will be experienced in trusting to God every dimension of loss which you experience. God has helped Mrs. H. W. to place her suffering experiences in their proper place in the fabric of her life.

She has the will to be happy not with circumstances, but above circumstances. She counts on a God who sees us through the storms. In my mind's eye I can imagine her active on behalf of others. I think she must also sing praise to God, even in the darkest hours of life.

EUNICE: *God Helps Me Bear It*

Dear Mr. Becton,

I believe I am most fortunate in having inner peace. I have just committed myself to the hands of God. I pray daily, and more often if I feel the need, that he will do everything for me, but of course His will be done in all things.

At the time of my surgery I prayed that everything

would be O.K., and of course it wasn't. I felt He had
let me down. I realize now that He had helped me
because it could have been worse. I have completed
six weeks of cobalt and have had five treatments of
intraveinous chemotherapy with five more to go. I
have had the side effects but not enough to keep me
from working.

Keeping busy has been a great help for me as it
keeps my mind occupied and I don't have time to
think about myself. I believe it has hurt my family
more than me. I had never been a person to be very
sick and I had always been very active and plan to
do so as long as I am able. But, as you say, without
God it would have been almost unbearable. He is a
great strength to me.

After I came home from surgery, at church one
Sunday the preacher made the statement that God
did not make bad things happen to us. He just
allowed it to happen and this was the devil that did
these things. But the Lord would not allow anything
to happen to us more than we could bear, for He has
an escape for all of us when it gets to the point
where we cannot bear it. So, death should not be
something to dread, because we will begin a much
more beautiful life that is eternal for which we are all
striving.

Sincerely,

Eunice W.
Texas

Hospital chaplains generally agree that four questions are upon the minds of those who face trauma and
tragedy: (1) Why didn't God prevent it? (2) Why doesn't

God stop it? (3) Why doesn't God do something? (4) How will I make it through this? Chaplains often find themselves attempting to explain something about "God's plan" as they respond to these questions. I want to explore these from the Scriptures, because suffering presents an urgent need to understand, at least to some degree.

Why didn't God prevent it? In John 11 this seems to be exactly the question the sisters of Lazarus wanted Jesus to address: "Lord, if you had been here, my brother would not have died." Their feeling seems to be, *Jesus, if only you had come in time, we wouldn't have this grief.* Many times, accidents that occur cause those who suffer to ask, "Did God not care enough to keep this from happening?" They may believe God cares and that He has the power to prevent. But He did not and their hearts cry out to understand.

We may seek to explain that God doesn't prevent it (1) because of the nature of the world He made (we aren't robots), (2) because pain and hurt sometimes have benefit, and finally (3) because we don't really know much about His reasons. The real issue becomes faith— what kind of God do you believe in? All ministry of comfort is based on the premise that God knows what He is doing, desires only our good, and loves us with unfailing love. He has conquered sin, suffering, and death; one day we will understand better. God's intentions toward us, because they are loving and good, cause us to choose to live and die in faith.

Why doesn't God stop it? Sometimes suffering people just want their pain to end. They are tired of it. Their endurance is exhausted. One sufferer asked me to pray that she could die, because she was so tired of it all. She couldn't understand what purpose or value her continuing misery held. If God was preparing her, she felt she was as prepared as she would ever be.

Maybe Paul's thorn in the flesh (2 Corinthians 12:7-10) caused him to reach the point where he wondered, "Okay, I've gotten the message. Now would you please take away this misery?" His prayers for relief were frequent and earnest. Apparently, God's greater purpose involved Paul bearing his affliction rather than being delivered from it. (Why do modern day "healers" ignore this?) Rather than the relief we desperately seek, perhaps we must lay down our desperation and rest totally on God's sufficient grace. This is a clear call for faith—because sufferers find no understanding of why it must go on and on. To declare, "God is with me in my suffering, working His purpose although I can't feel His presence nor do I have a glimpse of understanding why," requires a faith which only God can sustain.

Why doesn't God do something? Sufferers sometimes cry out for God to act, showing something of His loving purpose. Job wanted an audience, so he could catch a glimpse of what God was doing. God gave him no explanation, only a demonstration of His majesty. Sufferers often see things God could do to make their suffering, at the very least, easier to endure. Many experience frustration—a feeling that God has forsaken them—and that they must walk solely by faith. Let me remind those readers who may think, "This is obviously the way believer is to live," that it is far easier to tell someone not to be afraid of the dark than to feel confident yourself in the darkness. When the struggle for faith is your own, you recognize the power of both—faith and despair.

Sufferers must remember that God has a timetable, although they don't know where their suffering fits in. Faithful sufferers see the unseen and believe beyond their situation. The fire of one's suffering, like the furnace of Shadrach, is entered with the suffering believer saying, "He may not deliver me but I commit myself to Him." Many believers are able to testify to those around them in the midst of their suffering by being honest about how badly it hurts while at the same time affirming, "I trust God with my suffering; His will be done."

BONNIE: *The Joy of Answered Prayer*

Dear Randy,

I wrote to you in April about my little girl who was to have a mylogram and surgery in Milwaukee. She is now home and very much the proof of prayer being answered.

When she walked the first time we discovered our extra blessings. Thank the Lord, her right foot was straight and the toes were relaxing. The doctor didn't expect any of this to happen. This will eliminate about four surgeries. She had a great many prayers going for her and the Lord has showered her with so many blessings. We wanted to share our joy with you. I have been telling everyone about the power of the Lord. I have the living, breathing, smiling proof living in my home. No one can look at her and doubt.

Prayer has been so very important in my life. I could not survive without it. We are having financial problems right now. My husband doesn't have a job. If I couldn't go to the Lord, I couldn't go on. The blessing with Wendi made it just that much easier to bear.

In Christian love,

Bonnie P.
Indiana

Bonnie gives thanksgiving to God for answering her prayers by healing her daughter. Many times our prayers are for *deliverance* from suffering. This is appropriate. We also pray for *endurance* in the midst of suffering. This is wise. We pray at all times that God will *use* our suffering for His good purpose. This is worship.

But what do we do when He heals and restores? Are we grateful? Does praise pour forth from thankful hearts? Peter says, "The eyes of the Lord are over the righteous, and His ears are open to their prayers" (1 Peter 3). God's gracious hand of healing can be an occasion for us to be forever different. Every time Bonnie looks at her child, she will remember what God has done. The deep joy of answered prayer results in grateful living. This gift from His hand, the restoration of a daughter, is just another statement that God is real and active in the world today. Numerous believers who suffer have experienced the restoring hand of the Father. May we, as they, give praise to His name.

ELEANOR: *Images of Suffering*

Dear Randy,

Every time I try to write you I can do nothing but cry. I have cried over and over and there seems to be no end. I am 71 years old. I had four children, three girls and one boy. My first child died in her sleep when she was 24 years old. She did not suffer but it almost broke my heart.

My husband obeyed the gospel while in the hospital. He was there with four major strokes and doctors gave him up to die. In September he was taken back with another stroke and stayed nine months. I walked to and from the hospital (it was winter part of the time) and stayed most of the day and part of the night. It was a great problem for me to take care of him, but God gave me the courage and strength. I miss him so much I can hardly stand it and so, you see, I have two things to cry about. I live alone and if God wasn't here with me I could not make it.

While my husband was home with me for five months, I began losing weight. He insisted that I see a doctor. This doctor did not tell me I had cancer, but told my daughter who was with me. He sent me directly to the hospital for a complete hysterectomy. Two weeks later I went to a cancer doctor and in another hospital I went to take chemo—I go tomorrow for my sixth treatment. When all of this hit me, I could not understand, after I had lived all this time and had such a rough time, why cancer would show up. It almost broke my heart. I know God cares for me and I love Him with all my heart.

The chemo treatments make me deathly sick for a few days but I'm doing fine, the doctor says. It also brings my platelet count down and I stay so cold I nearly freeze to death. Also, my head feels funny. I itch a lot. But with all that he says I'm very fortunate. I believe with all my heart God is helping me. I think maybe He's not helping me and then I cry and pour out my heart to Him for help. May God help us never to doubt Him.

I realize my life is about over in age, and that I'll soon be going away. But thank God I'm a Christian. You don't know how sad it is to be in a house by yourself. Not a soul to say good morning to or to speak to.

I Christian love,

Eleanor S.
Georgia

There are several images of suffering in the Bible. One is the *furnace*. In Isaiah 48:10 God says, "See, I have refined you, though not as silver; I have tested you in the furnace of affliction." The refining process was Job's view of his suffering: "But He (God) knows the way I take; when He has tested me, I will come forth as gold" (Job 23:10). Peter tells those Christians suffering because of their faith that they are experiencing "grief in all kinds of trials" but their faith (being) "refined by fire" is going to result in "praise, glory, and honor" to God (1 Peter 1:6-7). He says these sufferers "participate in the sufferings of Christ" as they go through their fiery trials (1 Peter 4:12).

Another image of suffering is the *storm*. Job says, "You snatch me up and drive me before the wind; you toss me about in the storm" (Job 30:22). Jonah said to God, "Your waves and breakers swept over me" (Jonah 2:3).

A third image is *warfare*. Job declared, "He rushes at me like a warrior" (Job 16:14). Jeremiah said, "The Lord is like an enemy; He has swallowed up Israel" (Lamentations 2:4-5).

A fourth image is *travail and birth*. Paul said, "Destruction will come on them suddenly, as labor pains on a pregnant woman, and they will not escape" (1 Thessalonians 5:3). Jeremiah saw the invasion by Babylon as a "travail experience" (Jeremiah 4:31).

I think sufferers find these and other images appropriate descriptions of what they are going through. They know what it is like to be in a storm, or the battle, or travail, or the furnace. Eleanor identifies, I'm sure, with these images of suffering. She understands the power of the pain. Her faith continues, "I know God cares for me and I love Him with all my heart."

Her example helps other sufferers "hold on." Eleanor knows what John the apostle knew: "He (God) will wipe every tear from their eyes. There will be no more death or mourning or crying or pain, for the old order of things has passed away" (Revelation 21:4). She has "this hope as an anchor for the soul, firm and secure" (Hebrews 6:19). This hope causes the Eleanors of the world to know they are not suffering in vain.

VICKI: *Just a Matter of Time*

I have had surgery again and the doctors have said there is nothing more they can do. It will just be a matter of time. I am hopeful that through the prayers of my fellow Christians maybe He will grant me more time than the doctors believe I have.

I am concerned for my children. I trust that God will care for them when I'm gone, but the effects they are suffering now is what concerns me. My son is ten years old. He has been having nightmares every night. He's fairly mature for his age, and I wonder if he's put two and two together.

What I'm wondering is, Should he be told; How do I go about it; When should I do it? You may not have the answer, but maybe you know someone who does. My daughter is six, and so far I don't think she's picked up on any of this. My parents are

Christians and we have a good relationship. They will raise my children.

In Christ,

Vicki I.
North Carolina

The last great enemy is death. When a sufferer is told, "There is nothing more they can do; it's just a matter time," he or she then seeks to make necessary preparations. In Vicki's situation it involves the rearing of her ten-year-old son and her six-year-old daughter. She needs help in preparing them. Linda Vogel wrote the helpful book *Helping a Child Understand Death*, but the resources aren't really adequate to prepare a child.[17]

Death is today's "great unmentionable" for most people. No longer do children see loved ones in their extended family dying at home as in earlier times. Most often today death occurs in hospitals. Some children have been helped by the Concordia Press book which they read for themselves, *If I Should Live, If I Should Die*. This positive book speaks honestly to death's reality and hopefully to the presence of a loving God.[18] Vicki is prepared spiritually. She knows death's sting is over and that her death will transport her into her Savior's presence. She, like Paul, knows her life there will be "better by far" (Philippians 1:23).

BONNIE: *A Strong Faith for Suffering's Dark Hour*

Dear Mr. Becton,

I am taking treatments for leukemia. I couldn't see why God let this happen to me. I keep thinking God is stronger than the devil and He could have counteracted him and made me not have the disease.

I guess I should just thank God I'm alive and realize that I'm tempted no more than I can take. I know it's wrong for me to keep saying, "Hey, God, why did you let this happen to me?" But it is so hard for me to understand. Maybe I never will. I hope you don't think too badly of me, because I am trying and I know God is very disappointed in me.

I want to get back into a close relationship with God. So if you have any advice for a mixed-up kid (who should already know of God's love for her and that He knows best), please let me know.

I have so many conflicting thoughts. I guess that's because I know what I should be saying and thinking and I'm not doing it. I keep saying to myself, "You should be over all this self-pity (if that's what it is) or bitterness by now, cause at least you're alive and it has been at least six months since the worst of the problems were over" (that was my last stay in the hospital).

Sincerely yours,

Bonnie P.
Tennessee

Hard times call for a strong faith. But when hard times come, our faith often wavers so badly that we wonder if we have any faith at all. Bonnie told me, "I'm not sure I've doubted God's love, but I must have." The greatest challenge to our faith is not some atheist's comments but our own feelings when life doesn't match up with our faith. When things don't work out the way we believe they should (especially when we can't see "all things work together for good to those who love the Lord"), we wonder about our faith.

The person who wrote Psalm 73 saw things happening around him that didn't square with what he knew about God. So he declared, "My feet almost stumbled." It looked to him like God was not taking care of His people as He had promised He would. The psalmist even questioned why he should stay faithful to what he believed ("in vain have I kept my heart clean"), thinking perhaps it wouldn't make any difference anyway. Sometimes, when suffering people examine their experience and reflect on God's love, they may wonder about the promise that God cares for them.

There are some things believers can do to keep their faith strong in the hard times. First, I suggest that we not hesitate to be honest about our doubts. Faithful people can have serious struggles with their faith without being unfaithful. Psalm 73 shows that. God will see you *through* the struggle. He's not ashamed of you.

Second, remember those sufferers you have known or read about in Scripture who kept on believing. This helps keep you strong. Third, remember to worship God. Sing praises and pray—with other Christians whenever possible but alone if necessary. By reading Scripture you will remind yourself of God's love. Bitterness gets nipped in the bud when sufferers do these things.

If you can include at least one other believer in these experiences from time to time, you will eliminate the isolation and loneliness that lead to feelings of doubt. In this way you won't stay captive to negative moods. When I stayed alone in my own times of sickness, doubts and fears grew from small concerns into large and powerful enemies of my spirit.

The writer of Psalm 73 embraced his faith more firmly

after his period of doubting. He saw the danger in feeling sorry for himself. He expressed confidence that God would never leave him but would see him through. He ended the psalm by stating his confidence that God would receive him when the suffering ended. Psalm 73 gives encouragement to those whose confidence gets shaky. We all have those occasions. Let's be gentle with others and with ourselves in our dark hour.

JO: *Suffering's Strain on Relationships*

Dear Randy,

I am a victim of cancer. After four months of therapy, I don't even want to see or hear anything that has to do with cancer. Since March I have been sick, and the cancer was found in July. I am tired of being sick. I am used to being a very active person and I have no patience with myself when I'm sick. I am a nurse.

I guess I've often thought, "If God is allowing all this to happen to me to test my faith, then He and I both know I have little faith." I haven't stopped believing in God. I just don't understand why so much has happened to us. From March until the end of August I was only home 11 days. Sometimes I think I will scream if I have to look at another needle. Also, sometimes I wish I were not a nurse. I know too much.

My biggest problem is my husband. He refuses to accept what is happening to me or us. He won't talk to the doctor, won't go with me to treatments. He doesn't ask me how the treatment went. He won't ask how I feel. He is running from the problem and

I don't know how to help him. I'm dealing with a lot of hurt and anger. I don't push him. I love him deeply and I know he is hurting. But if ever there was a time when I needed him, it's now. I haven't said much to him about the cancer.

His folks say I have got to quit protecting him. They want me to tell him what I'm feeling and what the kids are saying and feeling. Our oldest son thinks Dad is mad at Mom because she is sick. I've tried in every way I can to make him understand that Dad is going through a very hurtful time.

This change in him has hit all of us hard. He told me today that he didn't like being around me after the treatments. I am trying to believe it's because he doesn't like to see me hurting, and not rejection of me as a person. I hurt a lot with pain, both physical and emotional. Sometimes I go to my room and cry until I fall asleep. I hurt so much other times that I get in the car and go to the mountains and cry.

I am not strong spiritually, physically, or emotionally right now. I feel like I am going to break under the pressure of the cancer and my husband's actions and feelings. I am grasping for any help to get him to walk with me through this ordeal—not to walk away from me.

In Him,

Jo J.
California

Suffering is often a family affair. Everyone is affected in some way, and each member may respond differently according to his own perceptions and needs. Jo's husband must not be criticized too quickly. He feels helpless. He is fearful that the one he loves will die, and he may even be angry that he is having to deal with his worry. It's not comforting to Jo, but these reactions of her husband are understandable.

Just when a sufferer feels isolated and fearful—just when he needs his loved ones to move close—the loved one may be fighting his own difficulties with the suffering experience. The sufferer may want to say, "I'm the one who's the patient; help me!" He may have to *comfort others* when he most needs *to be comforted*. Family members must fight against the tendency to withdraw in order to protect themselves against loss.

The changes that can occur require that everyone in the situation be aware of what's happening; they must commit themselves to communication. The tendency to be silent with our fears can be replaced with a willingness to risk talking about "it." We must be gentle with each other because everyone is an amateur when it comes to knowing how to deal with suffering and loss in the lives of those whom we love most. Everyone must adjust. Jo will understand her husband's sense of responsibility and protection for her. He will move through denial to the point where he gives her the strongest emotional support.

Resources are available to give care-givers (those friends who want to help) good information and suggestions for effective communication skills in situations involving illness, suffering, and grief. Dr. Neil Fiore's *The Road Back to Health: Coping With the Emotional Side of Cancer* is appropriate if the situation involves life-threatening illness. If the situation is loss, I encourage the reading of *All Our Losses, All Our Griefs* by Kenneth Mitchell and Herbert Anderson[19] or *Helping People Through Grief* by Delores Kuenning.[20]

Jo and her husband can be helped to walk together

through their ordeal. We can learn from them the forces that work on a marriage relationship when sudden illness strikes. Rather than allowing a devastating chasm between them to develop, they will recognize their diverse responses and differing needs. With God's help and caring friends, they can move toward each other.

JAY: *Assault on Self-Esteem*

Dear Randy,

I'm 19 years old, and my type of cancer is in the bone, localized presently in the thigh of my right leg. I'm on treatments (chemotherapy) now and will be for a year.

Sometimes I feel alone; a lot of times I feel angry, bitter, and depressed. My faith often wavers and this adds to the agony of wondering if things will get better, or if I even deserve for them to get better. A look in the mirror and a crutch under each arm (two years; crutches) doesn't help matters any. Of course, the look in the mirror had never been too gratifying.

When I first learned of my problems, I would sit with my Bible and hope some Scripture would jump out and explain why life was working the way it was.

Your friend,

Jay R.
Tennessee

What makes up a person's sense of self-worth? It is normal for a cancer patient's opinion of himself to be threatened by the disease. Often one's physical appearance may be altered by surgery or through chemotherapy and radiation. (Dr. James Dobson has studied the high value all of us place on physical attractiveness.) A patient may also find that people treat him differently—maybe as a child, perhaps in a "patronizing" way. If the patient has had a problem with self-assurance before the illness, as Jay indicates is true in his case, his fears and perhaps his anger will reinforce an inadequate feelings about himself.

We often forget how a person's self-esteem is tied to productivity—the ability to be mobile and to work. When our normal daily routine is altered because of physical suffering, feelings of uselessness creep in. Jay may face amputation at a very young age. This psychological assault on self-worth is very difficult (equally difficult for women who undergo radical mastectomy). At this point in his suffering, Jay must be given many messages about "God-esteem"—how much God loves him, accepts him, and thinks of him as valuable and unique.

Psychologists underscore that those who suffer from life-threatening diseases already feel a certain sense of uncleanness and unwholesomeness. When life crises hit us, one of the places struck hardest is our sense of well-being. We must have coping techniques—strategies to overcome. The sufferer must first acknowledge these threats and be receptive to the need for help.

Sufferers often discover the "law of compensation"— the countering of one's shortcomings by a concentration on one's strengths. We make adjustments in what we can do and we reaffirm that who we are is not solely determined by what we can do. We must say, I'm not important because I'm healthy, good-looking, smart, or productive; I'm important because of who my God is and what He has done for me. Those who serve

Jay should seek to minister to him in this critical area of need.

SUE: *What About Divine Healing?*

Dear Randy,

There are so many people who say, "If you had enough faith, God would heal you." This is very painful for me. I have had friends who did have faith and were not healed. On the other hand, I have friends who were healed.

In talking with my own minister some years ago about healing, he said he just couldn't bring himself to talk about divine healing with those "terminal" patients. He felt it was wrong to get their hopes up because if they were not healed, then they would have added emotional problems to their sickness.

In reading Scripture on the subject, some of the ones Jesus healed didn't even know who He was. Some people will not even ask for prayers for healing. It has been my observation that many people who are prayed for for healing have experienced added strength, joy, and a special peace which they did not have before.

Sincerely,

Sue
Indiana

It's painful to one who suffers to be told, "If you had enough faith, God would heal you." A heavy burden is placed on the sufferer when someone tells him this because he likely will feel an overwhelming sense of failure and guilt. Honest people who are desperate under their burden of suffering frequently are manipulated by charlatans and well-meaning friends who may be Bible illiterates in the matters of faith, healing, and God's purposes.

Does God heal today? Anyone who is careful with Scripture would say "yes" but with the honesty to admit that God doesn't heal everyone. The issue is not the amount of faith some desperate sufferer has, but the purposes of God. God's power cannot be reduced to some neat formula, bottled and sold, and marketed in his name. The apostle Paul thought that God could be glorified "whether by life or death." Are we so smart that we know everything about God's healing purposes? Isn't that presumptuous and offensive to God? I get angry when I see depressed sufferers who love God "put down" by the implication that if they had great faith God would heal them. Paul had a torturous thorn, a great hindrance to what he wanted to do in God's service. He begged God to remove it. However, God did *not* heal Paul. Why? Perhaps we must admit we do not know. There is much we do not understand.

Before me is a well-written book by a respected writer. He gives three "conditions" that must be fulfilled before a person can be healed:

1. The sufferer must want to be cured, must have confidence in God's power, and look to Him in expectancy that healing will result.

2. The sufferer must attempt to live in harmony with God's purposes and the laws of sound health, so that in the heart there is no obstacle blocking the inflow of God's power.

3. Sometimes the situation requires a "healing agent" who through prayer establishes a relationship between the sufferer and God "which the sufferer

cannot make alone." This mediator "is an instrument of the healing process."

This writer concludes, "Therefore, as you and I meet the conditions, we have every right to look to God for divine healing." This formula would be comforting if it were true. However, this formula has led to despair in the hearts of sufferers time and time again.

Sufferers (remember, I'm speaking of those who dearly love Christ) tell me "I must not have enough confidence. I must not believe enough." Or, they keep looking for the "right" contact man, mediator, or healing agent. Guilt and failure become overwhelming. God's Holy Word makes no such requirements. Jesus healed, on more than one occasion, people who seemed to show little faith in his ability to heal.

Who could qualify under point three above? Where does Scripture make provision for any mediator between God and man other than Christ Jesus? My anger is almost unbearable as I write this because of the horrible burden of guilt and despair in the lives of devout lovers of God. Please pray for God to relieve suffering and to restore those you serve. Yes, pray in faith because you believe He can do more than we imagine. But pray also for each of us, sufferer and non-sufferer alike, to be centered in His will for our lives. Whether we live or die, we are the Lord's.

GORDON: *Open to the Good News of Christ*

I am a young married man with a wife and family. My doctor tells me I have a terminal condition. I am in need of spiritual guidance as I find myself stripped of my health and unable to earn the money we need for so many everyday needs. Life has little to look forward to, for me and us. I am living on Social Security and a small pension from the Veterans Administration.

I have no way to go to church and feel confused in what to believe and look forward to in this life, or in life hereafter.

Sincerely yours,

Gordon B.
Vermont

This young man has come to the end of his resources. For perhaps the first time, he knows his need for God. Suffering can strip us of self-sufficiency and help us to see ourselves as we really are—needy, lost, and without hope. Paul described the Ephesians as being "without hope and without God in the world" before they became Christians (Ephesians 2:14).

Somtimes, however, suffering doesn't break down our pride and self-sufficient stance. When this is the case, we remain closed to the good news that Christ died for us and that He brings forgiveness, peace, and hope to all who come to Him. Sufferers who are Christians cannot imagine coping with their situation without Christ. He "abolished death and brought life and immortality to light through the gospel" (2 Timothy 1:10). He also lives within and encourages us in the midst of our suffering.

Gordon knows his need, and he willingly hears the good news of Christ. His life, because of his decision to become a Christian, will be new, *full* of hope, *with* God, and united with Jesus Christ. He has found the one security which suffering cannot threaten.

MR. AND MRS. R.: *Using Their Grief to Grow*

Dear Randy,

We lost our little 6-year-old boy a couple of months ago to leukemia. As the months go by and the shock wears off and the pain of missing him sets in, I'm requesting your prayers for me and my husband to have strength in the Lord and ourselves to continue on.

Mrs. R.
Tennessee

When the shock of a child's death wears off, the pain remains. It won't disappear, and it becomes a permanent part of the fabric of life. We are affected by all the significant losses we experience during our lives. Through them we learn something about ourselves, about life, about pain, and about joy.

Suffering can also be an occasion for spiritual growth. Many sufferers speak of growing spiritually as a result of their losses or difficulties. Some refer to their growth as a deepening of their spiritual commitment while others describe a renewal of their faith. They indicate suffering helped them to center their lives more completely on Christ. Maybe their particular affliction or burden strengthens their determination to trust in God. They perhaps experience God's all-sufficiency and surrender some of their self-sufficiency. If their experience brings them to their knees, then they may grow in dependence on God.

Other sufferers testify that a great loss taught them more about patience and endurance. Perhaps they experience a strengthening of the things they really believe in. Maybe it makes them more sensitive to the sufferings of others.

Suffering allows us to grow toward our goal, the "likeness of Christ," for we desire to be like Him in our faith, our priorities, our love for others, and our attitudes. Mrs. R. serves as a resource for others who have lost children. She is a sensitive, compassionate Christian who, with her husband, reaches out to families who grieve the loss of a child. They use their horrible loss as an opportunity for spiritual growth. I know families are helped by the caring outreach of this couple.

RONALD: *He Is There When It's Dark*

Dear Randy,

This morning there was a partial eclipse of the sun. Pre-scientific man feared the eclipse. They thought the dragon was killing the sun, their source of life. They were terrified, they screamed and beat drums, clashed cymbals, ran and hid, cried, and many other things, I'm sure. It passed quickly; the sun came back.

Now scientific men know all about the eclipse. They know when and where it will come and how long it will last at any given place. But we cannot do any more about it than our ancestors. It comes when it comes. After a few brief moments the light and warmth return.

Suffering is something like the eclipse. And it is not. It is like the eclipse because it is a shadow that darkens something precious or necessary to us. In the broad daylight of our everyday lives, suddenly the darkness envelopes us, and it grows cold.

Suffering is different from the eclipse because even though it usually passes quickly, sometimes it comes and stays. It is different because sometimes we cause it, and sometimes the cause is beyond us. It is different because sometimes we really can end it, or at least reduce it—sometimes.

Pretend that the moon could stop in place, and that the earth could stop its turning—a permanent eclipse somewhere on our planet. A circle of night a few hundred miles square, from now on. It would grow colder and colder. All the green plants would die. Probably after a while, glaciers would form there and scrape the rocks bare. It would be a place of cold death.

What would the people there do when it came? Before too long, they would realize it would not end, at least soon. Though habit, emotion, and sentiment would say "no", the only way to stay alive would be to move out of the eclipse, out to where the sun would still be shining, and life would be normal.

When some moon, known or unknown, eclipses some good that we need, want, and depend on and causes the shadow of suffering to enclose us, we must observe. Perhaps it will pass quickly. But if it does not, we must resolve to leave the shadow.

God is real; He is there. The only eclipse of God that there can be is when we decide we want to stay in the darkness.

Ronald

This is a stunning letter because of its deep thought

about suffering and its value. Ronald uses the analogy of an eclipse of the sun to describe the role of suffering in our lives. Those with whom I have shared this letter have found it a thought-provoking, encouraging letter which cultivates faith in God.

Scott Sullender says, "Belief in God, like all meanings, goes through a temporary eclipse in times of suffering." God is there even when our emotional moods say He is not. He is there when our reasoning about how life *should* unfold is not how it *actually* unfolds. He is there when the tempter says God has left us to our own resources. He is there when modern science can't figure it out. When everything is dark and silent in our soul, we can still *believe* He is there. Ronald has a unique way of coming at this truth: God is there and we can trust Him even in the midst of suffering.

CONNIE: *The Importance of Getting Help*

Dear Randy,

This letter has been in the making for a long time, but I've never gotten it on paper. I am a cancer victim. Mine was breast cancer—I had two lymph nodes involved, so am undergoing a year of chemotherapy. I've been very blessed by few side effects.

My Mom had a mastectomy in 1958, so I grew up with cancer in the family. The maternal side of my family has had eight cancer victims. Also, the fact that I'm not married, never had children, and am overweight has tilted the scales. At any rate, I feel that God has prepared me for this event in my life. I am a nurse, so when the cancer was diagnosed I knew what would be happening.

I've only been a Christian for three years, but the strength from the Lord and from my brothers and sisters really helped. The minister and his wife have been great. They took me into their home after discharge and cared for me.

It's frightening sometimes, because I have not experienced the usual emotions of a cancer patient. I've shed very few tears. Most people go through anger, bargaining, etc. and end up with acceptance, like we do with death. The last week has actually been my most difficult. I'm not sure exactly what the problem is, but I'm scared.

I guess I feel like I'm falling apart at the seams—I've been so temperamental. Two years ago one of my sisters in Christ developed cancer. We thought she was coping well, and a couple of months later she just fell apart. I'm so afraid that will happen to me—emotional breaks scare me more than anything else.

Four members in a church of 60-70 are cancer victims. One of us has died. Maybe that's what's scaring me—because I'm not ready.

In Christ,

Connie H.
North Dakota

Connie grew up with one particular kind of suffering around her—"the cancer experience." She went to nursing school to pursue the knowledge to cope with suffering, in her own family and in the lives of others. Then, the cancer statistics included her. She feels prepared, but she fears the mental and emotional battle even more than the physical battle. She worries about the loss of control and dignity that goes with cancer, but she also fears the emotional drain. She's having trouble giving her life over to God's care, since she fears it may end soon.

Connie feels she has so much to live for, so much to give to others. Her fear includes the feeling that she is not spiritually where she would like to be. Do we hear her? Would we take her fears lightly? Will we have the compassion to move alongside her in her fears, assuring her that God understands and that "it's all right" with Him?

Because of her family background, she has heightened awareness of catastrophic illness. Her nurses training equipped her with head knowledge, but it could not supply the emotional toughness she needs. Perhaps her anxieties have the upper hand right now. Her compulsive eating habits could be evidence of that. Maybe she's been concentrating on making "a good appearance" and staying "in control."

"Connie, you can't do it all by yourself," she has been told. She knows it. She is going to get help in dealing with her repressed emotions, working toward a healthier balance in her life. She is crying out for help, because her fears are the dominant reality in her life. She has been a Christian three years. Counseling therapy from a trained Christian professional will lead her to new resources for coping with her experience. I'm glad. It's a sign of great character strength to seek competent help when our suffering is more than we can cope with.

Over the years I have placed several sufferers with Christian professionals who are equipped spiritually and educationally to assist. Connie's courage should be an example for others. One of the ways our Lord helps us through our suffering is through His Spirit assisting us. The Bible teaches us about His comforting work.

Another way is mature spiritual counsel. God places within our reach many resources to help.

ROSETTA: *Whether I Live or Die*

Dear Randy,

I'm a 35-year-old mother of two children, 8 and 2. I have had cancer (melanoma) removed four times. Another spot regressed in response to chemotherapy in January of this year.

I had been a Christian over 20 years when I first learned I had cancer. I've been mainly concerned with the effect my illness, and possible death, would have on my children. Would anyone else, even a loyal, Christian husband, be able to guide them into a life with the Lord? To whom would my children turn with their problems of growing up?

For a time I assumed God's will was that I should die. I resolved to surrender to His will and thought for awhile that I was behaving as a Christian should. Now I know that I had really given up. My doctor tells me that the patient who does this is almost impossible to help. Then I remembered that Moses and Abraham changed God's mind. I would too! I told God that I wouldn't fight Him, but that I was going to fight this disease. With His help, I believe the common enemy could be defeated.

There are times, of course, when I doubt. I've found that these times most often occur in regular cycles and I can frequently talk myself out of them. I feel very good most of the time, except when I'm receiving either chemotherapy or immunotherapy. But the side effects of those treatments aren't as pronounced in me as in many others.

My husband has never doubted that I will get well, and his constant faith is an encouragement to me. Relatives and friends have also been supportive. Only one friend has withdrawn in confusion, but I know she has no intent to hurt.

Rosetta
California

God accomplishes His purposes in the lives of His children. C. S. Lewis wrote on God's omnipotence in *The Problem of Pain*. Lewis makes us aware of Scripture, which shows that God can do what isn't possible for us to accomplish or even fully understand.[21] But we must stop short of asking Him to be a magician on our behalf. This doesn't mean that, as His children, we should hesitate to ask Him for restored health. But we should ask according to His purposes. We know God has the power and will to intervene in His world. When He does, the unexpected occurs. Yet, it's true that sufferers with profound trust in Him sometimes are not delivered from their suffering.

What does a believer do, as suggested by the title of Robert Wise's book, *When There Is No Miracle*?[22] We continue to trust, being careful to remember that His timetable is what we should keep step with, not our own. "Those who wait upon the Lord" those who keep looking to Him—are not disappointed. I encourage Rosetta to fight on, in trust, and to pray that God will grant life. She is mature in her faith and seems to be seeking His will above all else.

I would encourage the so-called "faith-healers" to review the Scriptures again. These people would see the times when God is silent and does not heal. He always works according to His long-range viewpoint. Perhaps these people then would refrain from manipulating desperate people's hopes through short-sighted formulas for healing.

God does heal, but it is always according to His purpose. Also, according to His purpose, there are times when there is no miracle. I'm praying fervently with this young mother that God will reverse this situation and stop her illness. She will praise His name if this happens. I am also sure that if she does not get well, she will still praise His name. She understands Paul's statement, "Whether we live or die, we are the Lord's."

MOZELLE: *Power of a Fellowship Group*

I have recently had painful malignant surgery. I have a fine husband of 43 years and a bachelor son who lives with me. And yet I am *extremely* lonely to the point of asking for professional help. I cannot talk to these men I love. They are so helpless to understand. They are frightened and threatened, so I keep it to myself. My dearest friend, a sister in Christ, recently lost her husband. I can't talk to her about my loneliness. Yet we find time to share other things.

But my despair hits me so hard at times I almost wish I could. . . . I read the Bible many hours a day. My faith has sustained me so many times. When I am in pain I lose a great deal of my touch with God. For pity, I do not seek. A. A. has meetings to help people. Why couldn't we have group sessions for the lonely and the sick.

Only the person who has been where I am at this

time might want to listen to me talk it out. The
Cancer Society has a small booklet and a visitor
with a canned speech (a volunteer—and they are
something). But they are well and have no time to
listen to you talk it out. I have had several ministers
I respect highly. Mostly their answer is to pray and
turn it over to God. For two months I have tried this.
It helps.

Lonely, desperate Christian,

Mozelle T.
Texas

Mozelle recognizes her urgent need to "talk things
out" with someone and that only someone who has
been through a similar struggle would understand.
This is her dilemma. She must take a risk by reaching
out to her sister in Christ. Perhaps the fact that her
friend has suffered a great loss will provide both
Mozelle and her friend an opportunity to deal with
their feelings.

This letter points up what many sufferers have
mentioned—the power of loneliness. Her perception is
that she is all alone, that no one fully understands. This
may not be true, but it is how she feels. How important
are fellowship groups? They are *vital* in affirming the
worth of hurting people.

The President's Commission on Mental Health un-
derscored the importance of support groups in meeting
the needs of anyone in a loss or crisis situation. The
Commission called them a "first line of defense." The
task of absorbing the negative consequences of suffering, this commission concluded, is best handled by a
caring group. Perhaps one or two people are enough.
Those around the sufferer can increase his sense of

belonging, help him cope, promote self-esteem, and generally encourage good mental health.

We must add that each of us also needs a community of faith for encouragement. I have profited a great deal from Scott Sullender's discussion of churches as communities of faith and healing. He writes that when we suffer other believers keep us aware of God's love through their listening and serving but mainly by "being there." In the family of God, the suffering of one is always a *family* affair. When we care for each other our Heavenly Father is pleased.

SUZANNE: *The Limits on Our Service*

Dear Randy,

I don't believe there is anyone who has not been touched by cancer in some way—either personally or through a family member or friend. My own concern is as a daughter whose father has cancer.

I have two main concerns for my family. First, my sister and I live here in Iowa, but my parents and the rest of the family are a thousand miles away in New York State. Our frustration stems from the confusion of poor communication. My other concern involves the Christian faith. In my judgment, there is no hope if there is no faith, and so I feel that weight for my whole family.

I am seeking out anything and everything that may help me in sharing with my family.

Faithfully yours,

Suzanne G.
Iowa

Suzanne faces two challenges. First, she must encourage her father. Second, she must do it from a thousand miles away.

Many sons and daughters have asked me how they can serve a parent with a life-threatening illness. I remind them that a parent usually seeks to shield his or her child from the emotions of a suffering experience. Many parents seem reluctant to allow their children to minister to them in a significant way as they suffer. I'm not sure why this happens. One sufferer told me he didn't want to "bother" his daughter, for she has "her own life to lead." The desire not to be a burden seems to be common in these situations.

Another sufferer told me that a parent always thinks of a child as one younger and more inexperienced in the trials of life. I have received many letters from frustrated children who desperately wanted to help, but they felt the parents wouldn't allow them to do so. Of course, there are beautiful stories of how a parent and child "bonded together" in a healthy way during a suffering crisis, providing both with a precious experience. On the whole, though, we should recognize that it's not easy for a child to help in such situations.

When you add the complications caused by distance to this problem, it becomes frustrating indeed. Perhaps the following guidelines will help in such situations.

1. The relationship a child has with a parent *before* the suffering experience is likely to be about the same *during* the experience. Hope for a change (for the better) in a relationship should be a patient hope, therefore, with acts of loving remembrance and prayer as expressions of care. The crisis of suffering can help a parent and child to grow closer but this goal must be pursued carefully. Don't expect too much too soon.

2. Relying on intercessory prayer, written notes, and occasional calls and visits may seem unsatisfactory and

inadequate but, in truth, they can provide great comfort and encouragement. A parent may feel guilty when a child stops the flow of his life to come and stay a lengthy time. This may be necessary, but remember that a parent gives up his self-reliance and independence very reluctantly.

3. The sharing of one's faith with a parent in a difficult suffering experience may occasionally be effective, but I've seen little in my experience to suggest it. People don't generally embrace faith for the *first* time in the midst of suffering. Some do afterward. What is important is the *demonstration* of our faith, in acts of selfless service, as the sowing of seed. We must not impulsively seek to have a loved one "convert," for he will see our despair and worry and may feel pressured. We must realize that our agenda for another person may not be what they want to choose for themselves.

Suzanne can serve effectively from where she is. God has placed impressive tools in her hands. She should trust God for the changes that can happen. God, she must remember, loves her father with the greatest love.

CONCLUSION: 4

What Sufferers Teach Us

The letters you have read are only a few of the nearly 4,000 I have received over the last 13 years. These letters have pointed out several things that sufferers want us to know. I would like to summarize these lessons in this chapter. It is my hope that by knowing these things, we will be better equipped to help other sufferers.

One thing sufferers want us to remember is that it is intensely lonely. It doesn't really help that a lot of other people are going through pain. Suffering may come because of serious illness, a rebellious child, loss of relationship because of alcoholism or drug addiction, or a lost job. Whatever the arena of suffering, it is intensely personal and it is very lonely. Almost without exception the number one thing that people say to me is "It is so lonely."

They translate that in terms of a statement that follows: "Nobody really understands what's happening to me." Although we care and want to understand, suffering people perceive that we can't reach our arm far enough into the situation to actually touch them. I don't think this is always the case. But we're dealing with people's feelings about catastrophic events. The bottom can fall out in so many different ways. When it does, people often feel that nobody really understands.

The letters also show that people experience religious doubt: "If God really loved me, He would do something about my problem." To tell people that the Lord has done something about our sin, about suffering as a reality in the universe, and that he has accomplished this through giving His son may not fully console. They often want to know, "Will He deliver me today from this, right now?"

We all want deliverance from our problems. Of course, with maturity a person discovers that there are no quick ways out in some situations. There may be ways through the storms; but there are no ways to avoid the storms.

I have teenage children. One of the teaching opportunities I have is to show them that there are consequences to behavior, tough choices that have to be made, and horrible experiences that occur in life. "You will not go through this world," I tell them, "without being hurt." My experiences of loss and suffering are unique in the sense that they are real. But each person has losses that are unique to him. Therefore, it's important that we take a lesson from Jesus Christ on how to live compassionately. Christian compassion is the call of the hour.

Sufferers also tell me is that they fear rejection from those who love them if they do not handle their suffering well. They are frightened not only about the suffering itself but that they will be criticized if they don't handle their suffering well.

Dr. Ira North visited with me when he was fighting cancer. He said to me, "You know, Randy, from the soles of my feet to the top of my head I've believed in enthusiasm and I know that's what the gospel teaches and produces when we practice it. But here I am fighting this day after day. It's so hard to be Mr. Enthusiasm when you're fighting this difficult illness."

Can you get into his mind? With whom would Dr. North be comfortable sharing a despondent moment? Few ever saw him that way. We knew a confident and enthusiastic man. It was unnatural and difficult for him. Perhaps he had some concern that he would hinder other people's faith if they saw him struggling. But that, in fact, is a large part of the truth of suffering. You do struggle. You do face difficult days, and those days are not always victorious.

Sufferers want us to know that they often need a *visible reminder* that God loves them. They read the Scriptures. They pray. But with this almost "cosmic" loneliness—this loneliness that no one can quite break through—they need a touch, a presence. They need brothers and sisters in Christ who can, by their presence, serve as a visible reminder that God loves them.

This is why I recommend that sufferers not be left alone. When we're brainstorming about what we ought to do to encourage those who are coping with suffering, we don't need more ideas. We need to get in our car and go to them. Few sufferers will be critical of a person's words or visiting technique if that person shows genuine interest through his presence.

A man once told me, "I'm fighting bitterness, because from the day of my wife's diagnosis nobody has been in our house. It's almost as if they fear they will catch the disease." We talked for a long while and he said, "I know that they care, but they don't come." It's hard to visit when you don't know what to say. But we must. The call of the gospel is to be a visible reminder that God loves.

Sufferers tell me there's a certain fatigue to suffering. They are afraid they can't hold on. Now this is a little different than "I won't handle it well." This attitude is a weariness of spirit—a tiredness with the long-term situation. I'm thinking especially of physical decline.

A Faith Statement

The world has not seen any human suffering to compare with the only Son of God dying on a cross for man's sin. All suffering can now be viewed against the backdrop of his suffering event. When someone says they don't feel that God loves them, I understand their feeling. But my commitment is to help them to know it, whether they feel it or not. Remember, God is comfortable with the full range of human emotions.

The Psalmist shook his fist and asked, "Where were you when we were being devoured by our enemy?" He addressed God as if He might have been asleep or purposefully neglectful. Human beings who feel betrayed and abandoned have those emotions. The real danger of such emotions is that the sufferer will decide he is a helpless victim when the Good News says that through Christ we are victors.

A widow in California wrote to me, "My husband died and left me this apartment house, but I don't have any reason to live. I'm not mad at God but I'm hurt, so I just sit here all day and think about myself."

"Your husband would not want you to sit here and think and hurt," I suggested. "He appreciates how much you loved him. He would want you to practice your faith in God and to use your pain to bless other people who hurt."

Dr. Henri Nouwen describes the "wounded healer." He says those people who have been through pain and other difficulties are perhaps best equipped to identify with other people in their suffering.

We can suggest to sufferers that they offer their pain for God's use. This is best done quietly, one-on-one, as a suggestion that they think about and pray about. It can be painful to move from *being* hurt to *using* hurt to bless other people's lives, but I believe this is the intention of God.

Believers remind themselves every day that a loving God is in control of circumstances. He may not show a way around the storm, but He will show a way through it. The way through it is trust. Jesus demonstrates for all time that God cares, that He is present with us, and that He has defeated suffering and death. The future of believers is as bright as the promises of God. Believers live in that in-between time. Death and sin have been defeated—but it's an in-between time, as Romans 8:18-25 tells us, until God brings the fullness to His plan.

We can tell people, therefore, that we can't choose what happens to us, but we can choose how we respond to it. Dr. Baxter and I used to talk about suffering. He didn't talk much about his own, but he had compassion for me and concern for my family. "Randy, you and I both are privileged to know something that more people ought to understand," he said. "Whatever brings us closer to God we must see as good. And whatever takes us away from God we must consider bad."

Perhaps he was saying, "Sufferers have an occasion to reevaluate their priorities and draw their lives closer to God. It doesn't always happen, but it can. And sometimes, when everything's going well and the blessings flow, a person may forget his spiritual priorities."

We best cope with suffering by reaffirming the truths of the faith. The truth of the gospel, when embraced again and again, shows us the way through the storms. The gospel stands us in good stead for any difficult circumstances. We may greatly hurt. We may feel rejected or forgotten. But we can return to this one great truth—God is for us; He is never against us. He demonstrates steadfast love day by day, for all time to come.

Our Brother Jesus

The message of the Book of Hebrews is particularly consoling and encouraging to sufferers. The writer, inspired by God, says that Christ became a man in order to make salvation possible for us: "God wanted to have many sons share His glory. So God did what He needed to do. He made Jesus a perfect Savior through Jesus' suffering. The One (Jesus) who makes people holy and those that are made holy are from the same family. So he (Jesus) is not ashamed to call them his brothers" (Hebrews 2:10-11).

In Hebrews 2:14 the writer talks further about us: "These children are people with physical bodies. So Jesus himself became like them and had the same experiences they have. He did this so that, by dying, he could destroy the one who has the power of death. That one is the devil. Jesus became like men and died so he could free them. They were like slaves all their lives because of their fear of death."

Jesus came to help us by fighting our battles, especially the battle against sin and death. The writer continues: "For this reason Jesus had to be made like his brothers in every way. He became like men so that he could be their merciful and faithful high priest in service to God. Then Jesus could bring forgiveness for their sins. And now he can help those who are tempted. He is able to help because he himself suffered and was tempted."

Because these things about Jesus are true, we can continue to follow God with our heads held high and our hearts encouraged. Chapters 4 through 10 of Hebrews discuss Jesus' work as our Savior. These chapters show how his death declares the truthfulness of God's promises and his resurrection guarantees that God is absolutely trustworthy. Because of what God has done, we must now "hold firmly to the hope that we have confessed. We can trust God to do what He promised" (Hebrews 10:23). We are to follow Jesus' example: "Look at Jesus' example so that you will not get tired and stop trying" (12:36).

Sufferers sometimes experience fatigue. But Jesus' example allows us to go beyond fatigue with trust and confidence. We have a living hope that no suffering experience can shake. Because of this we can look beyond our own suffering and seek to encourage others who suffer. The writer says, "Remember those who are suffering as if you were suffering with them" (13:3). He ends the letter by declaring that "God is the One who raised from death our Lord Jesus" and that if we wait patiently we will be encouraged (13:20-22).

Perhaps my favorite part of Hebrews is the section beginning in chapter 4:14 and continuing through chapter 5:10. We are told that because Jesus is such a great high priest, we are enabled to hold onto our faith. The writer says: "For our high priest is able to understand our weaknesses. When he lived on earth, he was tempted in every way that we are, but he did not sin. Let us, then, feel free to come before God's throne. Here then is grace. And we can receive mercy and grace to help us when we need it" (4:14-16).

And then comes my favorite paragraph. This paragraph helped me in my darkest hours of suffering: "While Jesus lived on earth, he prayed to God and asked God for help. He prayed with loud cries and tears to the One who could save him from death. And his prayer was heard because he left it all up to God. Even though Jesus was the Son, he learned to obey by what he suffered. And he became our perfect high priest. He gives eternal salvation to all who obey him" (5:7-9).

Jesus is my Savior and Lord. He is my High Priest. He is the example for my own suffering. He is my brother. Therefore, I am never alone. I am saved from sin through His sacrifice. I can endure any suffering with His help, because He has overcome it all. I take all fears and all pain to Him. I keep trusting because I know He is working His way in my life. This is the message of comfort that suffering believers depend on. With Paul we declare, "Thanks be to God, who always leads us in victory through Christ" (2 Corinthians 2:14). We are led to victory over suffering, sin, and death through our brother, Jesus! He is the true brother of all who suffer.

APPENDIX 1

Prayers of One Sufferer

What do you say to God in the midst of pain? This short collection of prayers is one person's answer to that question. They express the thoughts and feelings that accompany suffering. They pour out bitterness, guilt, and fear but praise and thanksgiving as well.

These prayers come from the heart of one whose world was shaken by a life-threatening illness. You will probably see reflected in these poems some of your own feelings—feelings that you may never have put into words.

As you read these prayers, I hope you are impressed that the primary battles in physical suffering are emotional and spiritual. I encourage those who suffer to talk honestly with God about the struggle. He listens, understands, and cares. Remember, God deeply loves each of us. His actions demonstrate His love. Sufferers experience significant comfort and relief when they talk to God about their suffering.

I offer these prayers in the hope that these glimpses into my heart, in the midst of suffering, will help you. In doing this I pray you will move alongside sufferers, serving them in the name of Christ.

For You

O, God,
Give the best gift.
Grant health to return very soon.
Encourage me through the sharing of my own struggles
    with this my also hurting friend.
Be the perfect pillow for a very tired heart.
O, my Father, hear my plea for someone very, very
    special.

Show me what to do or say that will bless.
Grant me the insight and compassion of Jesus that I might
    help in some way . . .
If I can't help, Father, please do it all Yourself,
But help us both to know
    we are Your little children.
And we are loved,
Right now
    we are loved.

My Requests and Your Answers

Father,
I have sought so sincerely
For the gift of good health from Your hand.
I've believed strongly that I could then serve You more
    faithfully,
. . . helping more people
. . . being more useful
contributing to Your work being done in this world.

Your answers, Father, have puzzled me.
The gift of infirmity continues still.
Is this for greater glory for Your name?
Is it possible that I may do better things in Your service in
    sickness than I can do in health?

If this is Your answer, Father,
Help my strivings to cease and my heart to be calm.

Help me to trust that You know me best, and know best
   how my life may contribute to Your greater purpose and
   be a better vessel for Your glory.

Help me to remember, Father, what the point of life is
   after all—
Honor not for me—
   but for You,—
   the only God,
   of only love.

My Weakness and Your Strength

Father, I'm so broken in my health;
It's discouraging.
Discouragement and disappointments,
Doubts, fears, and pain
All cause me to feel so much self-pity that
I'm not useful, to myself or anyone else—
Not even You.
Sickness cripples my thinking as well as my doing, and I
   can't muster the strength to carry on.

Be very near me right now, Father.
I need Your strength—I need to know that Your tender
   breast was meant for me to lean upon,
That You don't tire of my dependence on You just to make
   it through every day.
Lord, help me not feel like a nuisance.
Wrap me tightly in Your everlasting arms—
Arms strong enough to hold me up every time I seem to
   be going down under the burdens for the last time.

I Can't Do Anything

Lord, I sit here sick,
Can't go anywhere or do anything I want to do.
I'm frustrated and downhearted.

I'm sorry to be complaining so, but it's hard not to feel
  bitterness
When my friends, who can go and do, try to console me,
When they urge me to be patient for better days when I'll
  feel stronger.
Will those days come?
It's been weeks now, and
I'm not getting any stronger.
The medicine doesn't seem to help.
My doctor says "it takes time,"
But I wonder if they all are just hiding the truth—maybe I
  won't get better.
This thought scares me.
Please help me think *clearly*, my Father.
I'm not ashamed I don't trust You more,
But I just must get better—please help me get better, to
  recover my strength.
I wish everyone walking around out there today knew
  what a blessing they have.
They can go and do.
I'm praying for that, Father.
I plead that You restore my health.

Complaining

Dear Father,
I never like to hear someone continually complain—
But now that's me.
Since I've been sick, I'm inconsiderate of those who wait
  on me.
I complain all the time.
I know it's not right.
Please forgive me. Please calm my Spirit so I can be
  gentler, and help me to appreciate the small blessings I
  have.
Help me to be greateful to You for Your presence.
When I whine, or gripe, or fuss,

Please gently rebuke me and help me see the dead-
endedness of this path of bitterness and self-pity.

Help me to think of others who are suffering greater pain
than I am and to pray for them and do any small thing
that I can do to lift their spirits a little.

When I complain, please keep on forgiving me.

I know You understand, but I also know how ungrateful I
must sound to You.

You've been so good to me.

You are *every day*!

Help me keep remembering Your goodness during this
sick time.

Fear for the Future

Father,

I've been sick for so long that I've started worrying about
my future.

I can't take one day at a time anymore.

I look far down the road, and I don't want the road to be
filled with bad health.

It was easier to trust You before the storm clouds gathered
and the hailstorm came.

It's been so long since my life has experienced the warm
sunshine that I'm beginning to wonder if I'll ever be
much better.

Will I, Father?

Please give me health again.

Please.

I know that You've heard my cries and felt my tears.

My heart overflows with hope that Your kindness will
once again restore to me sound legs and a healthy body.

Please, Father, more than anything,

I want to be well again.

But even now my heart knows that it should say—
"whatever Your will for me is, help me accept it."

I'm trying to say that, too, Father.
You know all the parts of me and the honest cry that
    comes from every one of them.
Thank You for hearing,
    for interpreting,
    for understanding every thing inside me
    even when I don't.

When I Hurt

Father, take my pain. Take it far away.
Sometimes I feel that I can't stand it anymore;
It's horrible.
I just lie here and hurt.
The pain medicine does not do very well.
In these times, dear God, help me not to turn my pain
    into bitterness at You.
Give me endurance.
If possible, give me relief *soon*.
Right now.
Please come quickly.

Time to Think

Father, I've been sick a long time.
I've thought about it a lot.
Our bodies are beautifully made but fragile.
I realize more clearly than many that the "outer nature is
    wasting away."
Even if I recover health, it's only a matter of time.
Help me to gain the right perspective about what to do
    with the remaining days You give me,
    whether long or short.
Help me be cautious about making a lot of promises I
    can't keep.
Help me to appreciate my health more if it is restored to
    me.

It's so foolish to treasure good health most deeply when
  it's gone.
Carve these things that You are teaching me now, Lord,
Carve them deep into my heart so that when You make
  me well again I will not forget what I have learned . . .
And I can serve You in a way I did not know before.

I'm Depressed

Father,
My friends say it's normal, since I'm sick, to be depressed.
But even if it's "normal," it's miserable.
I feel guilty, too, because I think I'm wrong to be so low
  all the time.
The doctor thinks it's just my body's lowness,
But whatever causes it, I need Your help.
Be with me in my depression and don't leave me—stay
  very close, my Father.
Please don't be too disappointed in me
I feel so helpless, worthless, and pitiful.
I'm so thankful You understand and love me anyway.
You are too wonderful for my feeble praise,
O God of the helpless ones.

Thinking of Tim

Father,
My hospital bed is tiresome, and the treatments are so
  terrible.
As I lie here, I think so often of "how awful it is."
Then I'm ashamed and repent before You when I think of
  Tim in that bed about six feet away from me.
He's in so much more pain.
He's so alone, with rarely a person to be with him.
I know You love Him—please, God help him; go to him
  and surround him with Your love.

Help me to say a kind word and quit thinking of how bad
it is with me.
When I consider the two of us,
I ask You to sit beside his bed tonight for I know You love
us both so much, but Tim doesn't know You and he
needs You so much.
Loving Father, please be for Tim tonight everything he
needs.

For Those Who Give Me Themselves

Father,
You know how impossible it would be for me to suffer
alone.
I need those who love me *near* me.
Thank You that Camilla is here.
Thank You that my friend is here.
Thank You for bringing one after another, quietly—but so
significantly—to just be with me.
You know me thoroughly, Father.
Thank You that I've met the loneliness of the battle with
disease *with You.*
I praise You for giving me these persons who with their
long, sacrificial, loving hours of presence have fought
the battle with me.
You know exactly what I need.
My heart overflows with thanksgiving for Your mercy.

Anger, Fear, Then Trust

Father,
Anger, even rage, fills me.
Not toward You, but
Toward cancer which seeks to consume me.

Anger soon gives way to fear and uncertainty.
Doctors and medicine—will they be successful?
In these hours I keep coming back to You, the only source
  of ultimate security that I know.
My life is in Your hands.
May Your will be done in me is my prayer.
Help my trust to grow deeper as the night grows darker.

Taking God for Granted

I confess unto You, O God,
I have taken Your gifts for granted,
Received them as if they were my "rightful possession,"
  something "deserved;" therefore, I've simply expected
  good health and a strong body all my life.
I was shocked when the doctor told me:
  "You have cancer, and it's serious."

Everything that I've assumed is up for re-evaluation,
But I know one thing: Life is *Your* gift.
I haven't deserved any of Your free gifts—including good
  health.
I don't know if I'll live or not.
How much suffering I may go through is uncertain . . . but
Regardless,
Father,
  Grant me forgiveness for my smugness, my insensitivity
  to the suffering of those around me, and my arrogant
  assumption that good health is simply to be expected
  rather than received with deep gratitude as a precious
  gift from You.

I now know.
I now know.

Illness as an Instructor

Dear God,
I've fought this life-threatening illness now a long time.
I would never have chosen this route to learn some of the
  lessons You've taught me,
But I'm deeply grateful that You've allowed this time to
  clarify my vision of life.
O, Kind Teacher, thank You for showing me the enormous
  need for loving service to others in Jesus' name, for
  helping me see how important people really are.
And I praise You for teaching me that all of us are
  terminal, but that through Your Son Jesus, we may
  share eternal life.
My days shall praise You for showing me that You and
  You alone are my security—
  not my job, my family, my money, my positions, not
  even my good health.
You have taught me, Father, in the school of illness, more
  of the real meaning of life than I knew before.
Praise Your name for Your use of great trials to refine Your
  children's values, especially mine.

For All—Praise to You, Father

For medicine,
For doctors, nurses, aides,
For prayers,
For cards, letters and words that are personally uplifting,
For a morning newspaper,
For a cup of cold orange juice,
For a wheelchair whose wheels roll truly,
For a kind lab technician who takes the never-ending
  blood sample gently—
For a window where I see the wind blowing the young
  leaves,
For a crayon card from my little child,

For a little better night's rest,
For all these, and all other *blessings,* Father, large and small
My heart pauses and turns heavenward to say:

I am truly grateful.
May Your kindness be my theme all through today.

APPENDIX 2

Things Learned from Illness

by Batsell Barrett Baxter

(Dr. Batsell Barrett Baxter was my teacher, then my co-worker, and a dear friend. We shared much in common, including illness due to cancer. He suffered a great deal without complaint and with great faith. He wrote this reflection on the value of his illness. I appreciate his giving me permission to use this material in my ministry to sufferers. It is included in this material so a wider audience can benefit from it.)

Back in 1964 a doctor told me I had a malignancy. That always comes as a shock; it is traumatic, but, alas, more and more common. One out of four Americans will have that experience sometime in their lives. One out of five will die with it. In 1964 an operation removed the malignancy. For something like 13 years, I had no problems. Then last year a second malignancy. I hadn't expected it; I was unaware of it. But it was real, and so an operation was scheduled in August of last year. On October 8, I was back for a repeat operation; the first one suddenly didn't work. The fall was a difficult time—much more difficult than 13 years earlier. In the course of it, I went through ten weeks in the hospital, something over $30,000 in expenses, and more suffering than I had had before. Out of that, I have learned some things—not new things, really—I just learned them more deeply. I came from it with a heightened appreciation for God's love and care.

Four Encouraging Scriptures

There are four Scriptures that stand out when I think of God's love and care. One is Romans 8:28: "To them that love God all things work together for good." Another is one that a great man mentioned as being most helpful to him some years back—Isaiah 40:31. It is not as widely known as the one I have just mentioned. "They that wait for Jehovah shall renew their strength. They shall rise up with wings like eagles. They shall run and not be weary. They shall walk and not faint." That passage really meant something to me. Another man mentioned Psalm 84:11: "For Jehovah God is a sun and a shield. Jehovah will give great grace and glory." And then this especially, "No good thing will He withhold from them that walk uprightly." That is a very reassuring passage.

And then I suppose my own personal favorite is Philippians 4:6-7: "In nothing be anxious, but in everything by prayer and supplication with thanksgiving let your request be made known to God and the peace of God which passeth understanding shall guard your hearts and your thoughts in Christ Jesus." That peace of God, that peace of mind, is priceless. And in that same chapter, "I have learned in whatsoever state I am, therein to be content." And then, "I can do all things through Him who strengtheneth me."

Increased Awareness of Suffering

In looking back over this illness, one thing that stands out is an increased awareness of the many who suffer. I have a greater concern for them. A little lady in her 80's in the next room who groaned in agony for two or three days is still in my mind. A young blind man whom I met as we walked the hall, getting the exercise that the doctors want you to get, was alive because he had a brother who loved him enough to give him a kidney. Suffering at the hospital is most apparent down where you get the x-rays because so many people are sitting in their wheelchairs waiting their turn.

Understanding Life's Priorities

I now have a clearer understanding of life's priorities. You know the point I am making. There are just a lot of things we do that are not really worth doing. They don't count for very much; they could be left off without any loss. I have seen my priorities a little clearer. I find I can cut some things that really weren't too important anyway.

Appreciation of Friends

Another thing I gained is a greater appreciation of friends. So many people did little things—cards, notes on those cards, the prayers of many people. One family, a family with three boys, took care of my yard. The youngest boy has taken care of my yard ever since. He didn't want any pay—just wanted to do it. There are just so many things; you appreciate your friends more because of suffering.

Greater Urgency to Preach the Gospel

I now feel a greater urgency to preach the gospel. Time is running out—for me, yes, without thinking of the other people. Their time is running out, also. There is an urgency to carry the gospel to people who don't know the blessings of being in Christ—or to people who only know it so shallowly that it doesn't really bless their lives very much. We live in a secular world—television, news, entertainment, business and industry, education—just a secular world. The pendulum of our time is swinging away from the spiritual toward the secular. But the same was true in Jesus' day. Religion was decadent. The Jewish religion was pretty rotten. Remember the seven woes in Matthew 23? Religion had become self-serving and empty. The paganism of the Roman Empire was rampant. How did Jesus tackle it? He did it two ways. One was by living his sinless life and the other was by carrying a message.

Those Who Follow God Will Shine

Daniel 12:3 has a simple passage: "They that are wise shall shine with the brightness of the universe." They that are wise are those who follow God. Their lives will shine with the brightness of the heavens. And then the rest of the verse: "They that win men to righteousness shall shine like stars forever and ever." And that is really the work in which all of us as Christians are involved.

FOOTNOTES AND REFERENCES CITED

1. Duncan Buchanan. *The Counseling of Jesus*. InterVarsity Press, 1985.
2. C. S. Lewis, *A Grief Observed*. New York: Seabury Press, 1961.
3. Neil Fiore, *The Road Back to Health: Coping With the Emotional Side of Cancer*. New York: Bantam Books 1984.
4. Donald Peel, *The Ministry of Listening*. Toronto: The Anglican Book Centre, 1980.
5. John Drakeford, *The Awesome Power of The Listening Ear*. Nashville: Broadman Press, 1971.
6. Peter Kreeft, *Making Sense Out of Suffering*. Ann Arbor, Michigan: Servant Publications, 1986.
7. Elizabeth Koop, *Encounter With Terminal Illness*. Grand Rapids: Zondervan Press, 1980.
8. Dennis E. Saylor, *And Ye Visited Me*. Medford, Oregon: Morse Press, Inc., 1979.
9. Elizabeth Kubler-Ross, *Death And Dying*. New York, McMillan Press, 1969.
10. Milton Meyerhoff, *On Caring*. Englewood Cliffs, New Jersey: Prentice Hall 1979.
11. Dietrich Bonhoeffer, *Life Together*. New York: Harper & Row, 1954.
12. Wayne Oates, *Your Particular Grief*. Philadelphia: Westminster Press, 1981.
13. John Claypool, *Tracks of A Fellow Struggler*. Waco: Word Books, 1979.
14. Mary Beth Moster, *Living With Cancer*. Chicago: Moody Press, 1979.
15. Leslie Weatherhead, *Why Do Men Suffer*. New York: Abingdon Press, 1960.
16. Elton Trueblood, *A Place To Stand*. New York: Harper & Row, 1969.
17. Linda Vogel, *Helping Children Understand Death*. Philadelphia: Fortress Press, 1976.
18. *If I Should Live, If I Should Die*. St. Louis: Concordia Press, 1975.
19. Kenneth Mitchell and Herbert Anderson, *All Our Losses, All Our Griefs*. Philadelphia: Westminster Press, 1983.
20. *Helping People Through Grief*. Delores Kuenning Minneapolis: Bethany House Publishers, 1987.
21. C. S. Lewis, *The Problem of Pain*. New York: McMillan, 1978.
22. Robert Wise, *When There Is No Miracle*. Glendale, California: Regal Books, 1977.